DO NOTHING!

STOP LOOKING, START LIVING

Damian Mark Smyth

Published by 3P Publishing, 2012
First edition printed in the United Kingdom, 2012
Printed in the United Kingdom

Credits:
Cover and internal design: 3P Publishing

Damian Mark Smyth is a teacher and trainer of the Three Principles. He lives in Berkshire, England with his partner, Victoria Groom and their dog, Wellington.

Photo: Rachel Harrison
RachelHarrisonPhotography.co.uk

Contents

Acknowledgements

First and foremost to the late Syd Banks, without whom, none of this understanding would be available to us now.

To the people who have pointed me towards this understanding. Without their words of wisdom, through the pages of their books, the hours of learning from their videos and audio books and their time, it would not have been possible; Jack Pransky, Jamie Smart, Cathy Casey, Sandra Krot, Keith Blevens, Valda Monroe, George and Linda Pransky, Amy Dalsimer, Aaron Turner, Mara Gleason, Dicken Bettinger, Garrett Kramer, Ami Chen Mills-Naim, Roger Mills, Judy Sedgeman, Bill and Linda Pettit, Michael Neill, Dean Rees-Evans, Linda Ramus, Mark Howard, Judy Banks, Rabbi Shaul Rosenblatt, Jo Hyams and all at the Tikun Centre. To Rudi and Jenny Kennard for their pioneering work in getting this understanding 'out there' through the Three Principles movies website,

For the inspirational writings and teachings of Vernon Howard, Robert Scheinfeld, Gregg Braden, Professor Cheng Man-ch'ing, Wolfe Lowenthal and David R. Hamilton. To Steve Jobs for his inspirational words, to Morpheus from the film '*The Matrix*' for saying what I already knew to be true but hadn't seen 'it' yet. To Daniel Priestley for inadvertently giving me the inspiration to write. To Emil Laslo and Sue Busch, thanks for all your help.

To Chantal Burns, Marion Jorgensen and the rest of the 3 Principles University team for their love and support. To all of the family and friends that believed in me and what I set out to achieve, thank you for your faith. To all of those who didn't, you gave me the inspiration to continue, because persistence and belief will always conquer doubt and fear.

To my ex-wife who was a great teacher to me, despite my not

realising it at the time! To my two daughters, Alannah and Aoife who are an inspiration and a daily reminder that being a child can be really, really good fun. And finally to my spiritual partner, Victoria Groom, without whose love and support I would not have been able to write this book. You are an angel sent from heaven.

Preface

The ideas I am about to share with you in this book are nothing new, yet you have probably never heard of them before. This book is a collection of teachings from many of the leaders in this field of understanding and yet you already have this knowledge within you.

I hope this book delivers them to you in a clear, concise and understandable way, one that points to a wisdom that you already have inside of you.

Because the title of this book is DO NOTHING! and as you may be about to learn, the best way to access what you already have is simply to realise you don't have to do anything.

My aim is to provide you with a reference, a quick guide to dip in and out of to help you on a day-to-day basis with issues and problems that on the face of it might seem insurmountable. By the time you have read and understood what is in the pages ahead, they will not only be surmountable but will feel effortlessly part of the joy of life itself.

Part of the learning and the journey *that is* life.

So dive in, let your mind wander, do nothing and start living your happy life.

Foreword

When Damian asked me if I would write the Foreword to his book, my first thought was, *"I'm honoured."* My second thought was, *"I have no idea what to say."* I had just spent a week with DO NOTHING!, offering some editorial suggestions, and I liked it. Which I admit was to my surprise because Damian is relatively new to this understanding. I also have my own new book in the works, so what could I say here?

Then, ironically, it came to me by doing nothing! I was soaking in the bathtub reading Keith Richards' book, *Life*, which I had been enjoying immensely, and somewhere toward the end he talks about his ex-wife developing a green thumb. He said the trees were being choked to death by ivy, so he gave her a machete and soon they were blooming again. The ivy had gone.

The thought came to me, *"That's it!"* That's how it all works! That's how it always works. The seed has been planted. That's us. The seed is meant to grow well and thrive. And it will grow perfectly, be in perfect balance and harmony, be aligned with the energy of nature, the energy of the whole universe on its own — unless we choke it off with weeds. And the only possible weed in this case is if we use our incredible power of thought *against* ourselves.

That's the only thing that can choke off the naturally flowing life force within us. And it's not even that we can really choke off the life force, because that's impossible, but we can certainly use this power in a way that makes it appear we're no longer connected to it. This is where all the anger and anxiety and worry and fear and depression and frustration and jealousy and fighting and wars come from.

But if we're the weeds, we're also the machete. To not allow our own weeds to choke us, we have the opportunity to cut them off at the pass and to clear them out. All we have to do is what this book says: nothing! All we have to 'do' is not take those yucky thoughts seriously, not take them to heart, not allow that kind of thinking to throw us off course and define our lives. And even if it does for a while, *"So what?"* We'll get back on track eventually, given what we understand (what you are about to learn) about how it all works and our minds calm down. This allows the life force energy within us, connected to the wisdom of the universe to flow freely once again – because it never went anywhere in the first place. It's our natural state... we can only get in its way, or appear to.

It occurred to me that very few things in life warm my heart more than seeing someone have a big insight, where they grasp how it really is an inside-out world, and then seeing that life change. The seed, the weeds and the machete are all seen at once. Whoa, we really have a grasp on it now! We understand! And that's how the seed spreads, one person at a time. And now, with this book, Damian will be spreading his own seeds of understanding... and that's a blessing.

I was struck by how good a writer Damian is, how lighthearted is his tone, how he uses wonderful examples from his own life. So read this book, enjoy, DO NOTHING! and see what happens. Who knows... perhaps the wonders of the internal universe await!

Jack Pransky, Ph.D.
Author: Somebody Should Have Told Us!
Moretown, Vermont, USA, April, 2012

Introduction

Have you ever wondered why when you walk past a playground at break time, or a nursery (pretty much any time of the day), you can hear squeals of delight emanating from every corner?

Children are a wonderful example of our natural state of being. They are playful, happy, joyous, curious, fun, excitable, delirious sometimes. So where did all that go then...? What happened to create the dull, grumpy, stressed, obnoxious, worry-mongers that most of us (walking down the high street in pretty much any town) seem to have become?

Could there be some other reason than: 'Well, we all have to grow up and go to work' and 'That's what life throws at us', or 'It's just what happens when you grow up'. Could it be that we are actually wonderfully happy as a default, even now in our adult lives but we have *chosen* to forget it? Could it be that we feel that we must react to circumstances when they arise? Could it actually be that we are doing this all to ourselves and we have been fooled into thinking all of it up on a day-to-day basis?

Well, actually... Yes! That is exactly what has happened.

You see, although it looks like the outside world is creating all of your inner turmoil, the truth is that it just, well... looks like it. It isn't real, none of it and I'm going to show you exactly why that is the case. More importantly, I'm going to show you what to do about it and the answer to that one might seem a little too easy and a bit too simple, but I assure you it is the right one. And you might well guess what that 'action' might be, bearing in mind the title of the book...

Firstly though, let me tell you about my own journey and how I came across this understanding in a very short period of time.

I won't linger too long on this bit, there's way too much other good stuff to share (like how to become happy like a child again!) but I think it will give you an idea of who I am, where I came from and how you can get the understanding that I will be pointing to in the pages that follow (which in itself might seem counter-intuitive).

My story started in September, 1969. Born to an alcoholic dad and a mother who married young as a result of an unhappy childhood, my upbringing was a mixture of huge rows and happy memories, holidays in the sun intertwined with arguments over spilled drinks and dog mess (don't ask). Not the best, but by no means the worst.

I spent most of my youth as a music obsessed 'Goth', listening to dark sounds to go along with the darker feelings inside of me. *The Cure, The Cocteau Twins, Pink Floyd* and *Marillion* were always on the Sony Walkman. Sometimes I even used a bit of *Motorhead* to get me going in the morning.

For all of the prophetic and wonderful music and lyrics I digested, I always knew there was something more to this enigma that is life – something bigger than all of us, something that no one could really know or describe. My parents called it 'God' but I wasn't going to be drawn into calling it anything.

As far as I was concerned whatever created the universe (as we know it) couldn't be described using words. I remember holding my Mum's hand in church one day, turning towards her and saying *"Do you really believe in this nonsense?"* I was about nine at the time.

What I didn't know then was that it would take me another thirty three years before I had even the slightest glimpse of what was *really* going on. Now don't get me wrong, I'm not going to go off on a religious path here (although some of what I talk about doesn't actually have form as such and is therefore spiritual in nature) but there are some pretty big questions that can come up on the journey of life such as: 'Why am I here?' 'Is there something bigger than our own existence?', 'Who or what actually did create the universe?'

Anyway, I digress. Roll on a few years and I am a successful graphic designer, have a beautiful wife and two children, a four bedroom house with a big garden in suburbia, stacks of friends and a loving family and yet... and yet, there was still something *not quite right*. Still a nagging doubt at the back of my mind that I was on the wrong path.

Then a series of what would appear to have been coincidental events (which I now know were not) brought me to a hotel in Heathrow with a raging hang-over, on February 26th, 2011. That's when my whole life changed!

I'll let you know how in a little while, because the realisation that led me to this series of events (and why I no longer believe in coincidences) happened only recently, when I attended a seminar in London, organised by the Tikun Centre of Jewish Wisdom. One of the keynote speakers was Michael Neill, Supercoach, from the States.

My new partner (not the ex-wife), Victoria was with me for the conference and at one point she asked me when I had first seen Michael on stage and I suddenly remembered something that happened six years previously which was the catalyst for the *whole series of events* that led me to writing this book.

My ex-wife was, at the time working for a large media company as their sales director. She was due to go on maternity leave to have our first child and being a canny young lady thought that her employment status would be improved with a little training, making her less of a candidate for redundancy. She was in charge of the training budgets so she put herself on a number of courses and NLP (Neuro Linguistic Programming) happened to be one of them.

One of the trainers that taught her was Richard Bandler and she suggested that I might get a great deal of benefit out of his teaching too. So I signed up for a course in London with Paul McKenna, Richard Bandler and (whom I thought would be) John La Valle. Only when the time came for the course, instead of John La Valle onto the stage bounded the aforementioned Michael Neill.

I had really been looking forward to seeing John La Valle, (the learning material that my ex-wife had given me was his and he was hilarious) but the way that Michael delivered his training was nothing short of excellent. His enthusiasm was infectious, his on stage presence was huge and he was hilarious as well.

As I was doing the training my spirits soared. I, along with many of the people on the course, started to think about learning this new technique to pass on to others.

But on the fourth day of the event, I was waiting outside the front entrance of the hotel and a taxi pulled up. Out of it stepped a dishevelled and downright miserable looking Michael Neill. I knew this look because my mother had worn it for a number of years in my youth... it was the look of depression.

That appearance of utter misery and dejection is more that just skin deep; it envelopes the very soul of the person it holds. It is by no means an easy sight to see, there is a sense of helplessness for the voyeur. I remember at the time thinking: how could this new technique (NLP) be so fantastic, if the people teaching it weren't benefitting from it? There was something incongruent about the whole thing.

Weeks later, when the feeling of elation from the course had died down, I heard on the grapevine that a number of people on my course were indeed taking NLP up as their new profession but I made the decision not to do the same. If it was *that* good, surely it would be good for everyone. Basically, it just didn't *feel* right.

My own seeker's journey therefore continued: Tai Chi, Yoga, Meditation, Buddhism, Hypnosis, the list continued to grow. Roll on a few years and I went to another Michael Neill event in London. This time, he was doing a day's workshop on '*Relationships with Money*'. Mine, at that time was not a good one. Well, it would have been nice to have had some, so at least I could have started one!

When I saw Michael at this event he looked quite different. He was more at ease with himself and he didn't talk about NLP at all this time. I was curious about what had happened to him since our last meeting back in 2005.

It was also at this event that I met Jamie Smart for the first time – Jamie introduced me to the Principles I will refer to in this book some three years later on down the line. We got on well and I liked his demeanour and something in the back of my mind told me to keep in contact with him, so I signed up for Jamie's NLP tips through his company *Salad*.

I continued to follow NLP, despite my misgivings about it's efficacy, but there were very few trainers that I continued to keep tabs on and for some reason I kept up with Jamie and his weekly tips and newsletters in the following weeks, months and years.

So it was in early 2011 that I received an invitation email to one of Jamie's events called *'Getting Clients Congruently'* where I would hear about this new understanding for the very first time. By this stage my (still then) wife and I had decided that a trial separation was the way to stop the constant arguing and I was about to start a new job away from home in Newbury, Berkshire. The idea was that, if we could not resolve our differences we would make the split permanent and by that stage our two girls would be comfortable with Daddy living away from home. I moved into a business development role with a design agency in Newbury and seeing that Jamie's event was about getting clients (sales) effectively, I made the booking.

That chance peek at Michael Neill in 2005 and not following the NLP route, which in turn led me to meet Jamie and discover the Principles that I am about to share, has also led me to find my spiritual partner, who also found her own path assisted by Michael – Ironically, we later discovered that I was at another Michael Neill event in 2010 sitting at the very back and Victoria was at the same event sitting at the very front. Our paths were starting to converge...

It was at the Tikun event in London which I mentioned earlier, where Michael described his battle with depression. He told how he used every technique under the sun to disguise his true self to others, until he discovered the Principles that is. Then I remembered that dishevelled looking man stepping out of the taxi cab back in 2005 and it all came flooding back to me.

He was the reason that I chose to wait and not follow the NLP path. He was the reason that I met Jamie Smart. He was the reason that I came to know about the Principles. He was the reason I met Victoria. He was instrumental in my understanding of this new paradigm and why I am writing this right now. How intriguing!

And so it was on that cold winter's morning back in February, sitting in the fourth row from the stage with that hangover – that I really *heard* something. The fact that I was not properly *listening* was most likely the reason why I heard something beyond the words being spoken.

Something resonated and touched me at a deeper level right into my core. Something made sense out of all of the seeking that I had been doing and had eluded me for all those years. It was something so simple and yet so profound that it literally stopped me dead in my tracks. This pointed to an understanding of life that was way bigger than I could possibly imagine, yet was really so very gentle and true. This was the something that *explained*, for want of better words, *what I had been looking for* – the missing piece in the jigsaw that made up who I was, who I am and who I will always be.

As I started to unravel the simple truths that I will reveal to you in this book, I soon realised the sheer immensity of the puzzle. I was only scratching the surface of something that was so profound and so beautiful. Over time and with the help of many of the amazing teachers mentioned in this book, my understanding of the Principles deepened and my life became better as a consequence.

Then on one weekend back in July 2011, I had the pleasure to attend a two day workshop on the Principles with Jack Pransky and Amy Dalsimer. Jack's book: *Somebody Should Have Told Us!* was the first book that I had read on the Principles and is my 'go to' book for anyone who wants to know more about this understanding. Those two days spent with Jack and Amy changed my whole outlook and my own purpose in life. I knew, walking away up the road from that workshop that I had to take this understanding and pass it on to as many people as I could, so I started to ponder how this could be done.

It soon occurred to me that there was not one single book which summarised ALL of the subject areas of this understanding. There were numerous books on various areas; relationships, sports, parenting, but none that had practical examples of *everything* in one place. So I began to collate the information that I had gathered from the trusted sources, writers and teachers who had been spreading the word of the Principles for many years. In a moment of clarity (and asking for guidance) the answer was given to me: in all cases, the way to achieve our natural state of happiness is to do nothing! If you let the thinking go, the clouds naturally move out of the way and the sun will reappear, because it is always there – even when we think it isn't.

So I decided to use this premise as the vehicle to deliver my own understanding to you in the following pages. Because when it comes right down to it, there really is nothing to do. It seems too simple to be true but then again the simplest explanation is often the right one, as Einstein said.

The teachings that follow in these pages are all taken from real life events, some of which involve me, others involve friends or my teachers or the clients of the people mentioned in the acknowledgements. All of them are part of the understanding that I will try to convey to you.

I must emphasise something here: the words within this book merely allude to something, *they are not the thing itself.* Words are form and the *truth* is formless; the map is not the scenery.

What I have put together here is just the tip of the iceberg. If you can get a feel for what I am trying to convey, then I will have done my job. There is a list of source material at the back of the book with which I highly recommend that you continue your learning. If you even get just a glimpse of what I refer to here, you will know that your own learning will never cease.

In the meantime though, let me just leave you with this thought before you dive in. It is in every chapter, every sentence and every message that I have written:

You are already perfect, there is nothing to do, nowhere to go, you already have all the answers. DO NOTHING! and they will emerge.

Damian Mark Smyth
Eze, Côte d'Azur, France
May, 2012

Chapter One

Preparing for a new level of understanding

Morpheus: "What you know you can't explain, but you feel it. You've felt it your entire life, that there's something wrong with the world. You don't know what it is, but it's there, like a splinter in your mind, driving you mad."

Have you ever had the feeling that there is more to something than meets the eye? Of course you have. You won't have gone through your life without hunches – you know, the nagging doubt in the back of your mind that all was not as it seemed: that boyfriend who was not quite right for you, the way to work that, for some reason *on that particular morning* seemed wrong and unbeknownst to you there was a pile-up ahead. Can you explain those?

Yet when we reach adulthood, we hold onto this stubborn view that we know it all. Can you really actually, hand on heart say that you do *know it all*? Of course not! If you did (or do), then please explain the origins of the universe to me. What was there before the big bang? In fact, whilst you're there, tell me why the universe is expanding and speeding up in the process, against all the laws of physics that we currently know about*.

Yes, let's start with something really easy! My point here is of course, that you do not know everything. No one does. No one probably ever will. What is 'everything' anyway? There are things in life that we simply cannot explain yet. What is the missing 96 percent of the universe made of? That 'dark matter' as it's called,

---

*The Nobel Prize in Physics 2011 was divided, one half awarded to Saul Perlmutter, the other half jointly to Brian P. Schmidt and Adam G. Riess 'for the discovery of the accelerating expansion of the universe through observations of distant supernovae'.

is definitely there but we can't see it. We can't even measure it, but we do know it's there.

Yet, when it comes to understanding something entirely new, most of us tend to hold onto what we already know. It's got us here, so why should I choose to think something else? It's the filter through which we communicate with the world. Everything we do in fact, is filtered through what we already know. This is why when you heard mathematics taught at school for the first time, unless you were a genius, it would have seemed like a bit of a mess of ideas thrown at you by the teacher. It probably wasn't until much later on down the learning path that you *saw* what was being taught for the first time, where you actually realised that you didn't have to memorise the adding, subtracting etc, but could simply do it with the process or formula. You were awakened to a new level of understanding – and how much easier was that... to 'do'?

Some of what I am about to allude to in the following pages might seem as if it is similar to other types of ideas you are already aware of, *but I can assure you that it is not.* In fact, there is a great story about this: One of my teachers, Jamie Smart tells his own story at his seminars and events of the time that he was shown this new understanding some 12 years ago, took one look at it and said: *"Yup, I know that already... in fact the stuff I'm doing is way cooler"* (he's from Canada). Some nine years later he was pointed to this learning again, and had a similar response: *"Yup, I was right, that's b*llocks"* (his words not mine). It was only two years after that, when he was being taught by Michael Neill (told you he was pivotal) who explained to Jamie that all of his learning would be done using this particular understanding, that he sat up and took notice. Realising that he might have missed something, he went back for another look. Two years later and this is the primary understanding that Jamie uses to teach with. He thought he knew, but he was filtering through what he already knew. Big difference.

Throughout history, there have been new discoveries that have shocked and challenged the current thinking at the time. In many cases, the scientists, doctors, astronomers and biologists who discovered them were vilified by their professions and cast out into the wilderness.

In the case of Ignaz Philipp Semmelweis, for instance, who discovered that diseases were caused by tiny invisible creatures that lived on our hands (and not by bad smells, which was the current thinking at the time), he was thrown into the asylum where he perished of the very thing he was trying to prevent! The term *'Semmelweis Effect'* relates to the time lag required for any new understanding to take hold.

A perfect illustration of this very effect is the sad story of James Abraham Garfield, the 20th President of the United States of America. You may not have heard of him, because Garfield's presidency lasted a mere 200 days from March 4, 1881, until his death on September 19, 1881, as a result of being shot by an assassin, Charles Guiteau on July 2, 1881.

The interesting thing about this historical incident, is that Guiteau denied killing Garfield in court. You see the two shots that Guiteau fired did not actually kill Garfield directly. One bullet grazed Garfield's arm; the second bullet was thought later to have been lodged near his liver but could not be found (and upon autopsy was located behind the pancreas).

Garfield became increasingly ill over a period of several weeks due to infection and on Monday, September 19, 1881, he suffered a massive heart attack and died, some eighty days after the shooting.

According to modern medical experts, Garfield would have survived his wounds had the doctors attending him fully accepted the sterilisation techniques implemented by Joseph Lister during the 1860s – some 20 years earlier! Because standard medical practice at the time dictated that priority be given to locating the path of the bullet, several of his top doctors inserted their unsterilized fingers into the wound to probe for it! Now these were the *leading* doctors and surgeons at that time. They were working for the President of the United States of America and yet they still believed in outdated practices. They actually held the firm belief that having a dirty operating room was the sign of a good surgeon! I mean... I ask you?!

There are in fact so many cases of new ideas being ridiculed by the masses, that to go through them would be a whole book in itself: Galileo, Copernicus, Louis Pasteur are all great examples of this. My point here being: just because an idea doesn't sound like it's feasible, doesn't mean that it isn't.

So I would like to offer you a suggestion. When you read the pages that follow, try to read from a place of 'not knowing'. In fact, might I suggest that the very reason you are reading this book is because your current level of *knowing* has not necessarily brought about the ultimate results you desire in your relationships, business, family or career. There might be a reason for this, so don't hold onto it too tightly!

To use another metaphor, when you listen to music, do you listen for all of the breaks, notes, drops, middle eights and so on, or do you listen for the overall feel of the piece and the message it conveys? Might I suggest that you do the same when you read this book – but do the reading equivalent of listening to music – whatever that is! There's a good chance that you might hear something beyond what you already know.

Now I got all of this new understanding from essentially doing nothing! I simply let go, and the answers emerged. I stopped listening or reading for agreement or disagreement, I just stopped doing anything. The understanding came from a different level of thought – a different level of consciousness. Yet when it came, it seemed so obvious. How many times has that happened to you, when an answer came from (seemingly) nowhere to a problem that needed solving? *"We can't solve problems by using the same kind of thinking we used when we created them,"* as Einstein said.

What I am alluding to here is that if you listen (or read) from a point of view of *not knowing* and you are prepared to agree that there is an understanding out there which *might* be of use to you in some shape or form, then we are ready to rock and roll!

The best part of it is of course, that you do nothing! It'll come when it's ready... so let it come.

Chapter Two

The Three Principles (part 1)

"Thought is not reality; yet it is through thought that our realities are created" – Sydney Banks

In 1973, Sydney Banks, a minimally educated welder from Edinburgh in Scotland had a profound experience, leading to an insight that catapulted him from being an insecure, unhappy man into one of the world's leading theosophers, lecturing to universities and professors as well as professionals in the fields of social work, law enforcement and business around the globe. The one thought that he had on that day gave him an understanding of the workings of the universe, our place in it and how we navigate our way through life.*

The story goes something like this: According to Syd's own verbal accounts*, he and his wife Barbara went to a relationship seminar held on Cortes Island in British Columbia, Canada (but not without signing up and then cancelling several times through fear and insecurity). This particular seminar encouraged couples to let their feelings out, be honest and argue with one another openly. The couple were unhappy with this process and Syd and Barb (as she was known) prepared to leave the seminar to journey back home. Before they left however, Syd, who described himself as an insecure mess at the time, engaged in a conversation with a psychologist who was also attending the seminar with his wife, as a delegate. They got talking over a coffee and the psychologist asked Syd about his problems. Syd told the psychologist that he was really insecure and

---

*I would highly recommend that you hear Syd's own words, in his own voice, describing his experience. 'The Experience' DVD from the Long Beach Lectures is available from Lone Pine Publishing: www.lonepinepublishing.com

elaborated on all the ways why he felt like this. The next day, Syd and Barb bumped into the same psychologist and his wife who said that what Syd had told him the previous evening was total nonsense and Syd was not really insecure, he just *thought* that he was.

Now, what Syd heard the psychologist say at that very moment was: *'There's no such thing as insecurity, it's all just thought.'* All of his insecurity was *only* his thinking! It was like a bomb going off in his head. He described it as being enlightening and totally unbelievable, so he asked the psychologist if he realised what he had just said. At this point the psychologist became all insecure and told him that *"Of course he realised what he had just said or he wouldn't have said it"*. But Syd saw that he could not have fully understood his own words otherwise he would not have reacted in this way. Syd had heard the words at a much deeper level than had been spoken to him.

In the following three days after he had had this awakening experience, Syd began to see truth after truth about the universe and the way that we navigate our way through life. He barely slept, as all of the information from this higher place came into him. He went to his mother-in-law's house (with whom he did not get on) and overheard his wife and her complaining about how happy Syd has been in the past few days, which he found incredibly funny. He laughed so loudly that his mother-in-law heard him and confronted Syd and asked him what he found so funny. Syd, worried that he had offended her, looked out of the window, and at that moment saw what he described as a buzzing white light – the transcendent light of knowledge dawning upon him and he realised that God (or Spirit) was everything and everywhere. As soon as he saw that, he realised the true nature of 'Universal Mind', that it is the *formless pre-existing energy of everything.*

Syd saw that there are three formless Principles of Mind, Thought and Consciousness which explain the whole range of human behaviour and feeling states. In Syd's words: *"They create all human experience."*

He defined the Three Principles in his books as follows:

> <u>Mind</u> *is the energy and intelligence of all life, whether in the form or formless. The Universal Mind, or the impersonal mind is constant and unchangeable. The personal mind is in a perpetual state of change.*

> <u>Thought</u> *is a divine gift, which serves us immediately after we are born. It is the creative agent we use to direct us through life. It is our rudder to steer us through life.*

> <u>Consciousness</u> *is the gift of awareness, it allows the recognition of form... form being an expression of Thought.*

Syd turned to his wife and mother-in-law and said that what he had just learned would mean that he would be speaking to universities, lecturing to doctors and writing books and that their whole lives were about to change. Now this worried them greatly because here was this ninth grade educated welder, who couldn't even spell psychologist, let alone teach one, making these bold assertions about the future! But Syd saw it and *it happened precisely the way he envisaged.* He saw clearly that he would be spreading the word about these Three Principles to the world for the rest of his life.

Syd's primary thought was, 'Who am I going to tell first'? He went to tell the pastor on the island that he lived on in Canada, presuming the pastor would tell the bishop and the bishop would tell his superior and eventually it would get to the media. That way, Syd thought, soon humanity would be able to see the innocence and blindness of the ego and we would all wake up to the 'truth'... that the whole world would take stock and heal from within itself. What Syd did *not* reckon with, is that we all see things through our own filters and that each person's ego needs to be hurdled to get to a place of openness – to this new level of thinking. Essentially, Syd was not telling anyone anything new, he was just talking to them about a level of understanding that we can all see for ourselves, if we look inside our souls.

Which brings me back nicely to the title of this book: DO NOTHING! There is no technique, no process, nothing to do, nowhere to go, it is purely and simply an understanding that *is* truth. It is what this world is *made* of, not merely what we *see*. Everything is a manifestation of Mind, Thought and Consciousness. *Everything*!

Think about it now. What are you doing *right now*? If you are reading this, you are using your Mind (some sort of intelligent life-force running through you), Thought (thinking, 'what's he on about?'... or not) and Consciousness – you are aware of it, I hope(!) and feeling something. So in actual fact, there is nothing you can perceive in this world that does not come through the Three Principles. If you can give me an example of anything that does, please, please... tell me. If you are thinking, 'No, he's wrong about that'... you're using the Three Principles *to have that very thought*. Everything that you have ever done, experienced, lived, thought, tasted, smelled, loved, hated, whatever it is... has come through these Principles, because if you have lived it, thought it and felt it... you've used Mind, Thought and Consciousness in the process.

Someone asked me recently at a training day, *"But what about someone in a vegetative state on a life support machine. They're not using these Principles are they?" "Good point"* I replied. *"So tell me, what reality are they experiencing?" "Not much of one, I guess"* was the response. Anyone's reality can only ever be created via these Principles. What a great example! We really have no idea whether someone in a vegetative state is experiencing any thoughts or not, but it is very possible that at some very low level, thoughts may still exist. But at whatever level it is, we can be fairly certain that consciousness is picking up whatever thoughts *are* being generated and if it is at an extremely low level, then that is the 'reality' that they are experiencing.

Now earlier I mentioned that Sydney Banks uncovered them. There's a very good reason for choosing this word, because like gravity, they have always been here. Gravity didn't just start happening when we discovered it. No, it has always been working and always will and it works the same on you as it does on me. This is the reason that we call them 'Principles'. A principle is something that is true whether you believe it or not, whether you understand it or not. It is an *essential characteristic of the system.* So the Three Principles are there. How we use them is up to us and most of us, oblivious to the fact that this is how the system works, use them pretty badly!

What happens next is the really exciting part, because hopefully you get some sort of an idea of what's going on here by now. *You create everything in your reality through the Three Principles of Mind, Thought and Consciousness from moment to moment.* <u>You</u> are the one who is responsible for this, <u>no one else</u>. By merely having an understanding of this, you have raised your own level of awareness (consciousness). So how can you use this increased awareness to be able to live a better life?

Let me start first by giving you a quick example of how having an understanding of something might benefit you: When I was a boy, my dad used to live in Brazil on the coast, in a small town called Ubatuba, which was located just north of Sao Paolo. There was a beautiful beach there with crisp white sands and wonderful rolling waves. What he didn't know was that at certain times of the day there was a very strong current in the water which, unless you were an expert swimmer, would drag you far out to sea in a matter of seconds. When my father first arrived there he had no idea about this. It was only when he was about to go for a swim one day that a local man stopped him and told him about the danger. He could have found out about it the hard way, but he was pretty thankful that he didn't have to. Having an understanding about how the tides worked helped save him from danger. There was nothing he could 'do' personally about the tides, they were always there, working day and night without his help. But having an *understanding* about how they operated was vital.

By having a basic understanding that this is how our minds work, how our thinking works and how are realities are put together, it gives us more freedom and dare I say it... saves us from danger! *All mental and feeling states are self-created through thought – all of them.*

You don't have to learn what to do with the mind, because thought is essentially just a form of energy that shows up in your head. If you don't put more energy into it, it will change and roll on by like the waves on the ocean. They move and shift, you don't have to do anything with them. The degree to which people's thinking freaks them out or they think that it's not being created from inside of them, is the degree to which they will splash around in it, creating more waves and more freaked out thoughts. Sound familiar?

The truth is, most people believe that their thoughts *are* reality and this reality is somehow created by what's *outside of us*. It's not surprising really is it? We've been told this all our lives. The media every day point to an 'outside-in' world where our happiness (or unhappiness) comes from our circumstances. *"Buy this to feel better! Get rid of that to have a great life! These people are out to get you — but these people will save you from them."* It all looks like what's *out there* is the reason for what's going on *in here*, but thoughts and feelings *only ever* come from inside of us and *always* through the Principles.

Let me use an example to show you this. There are at the time of writing, just over seven billion people on the planet. That's a lot of opinions, don't you think? So if I were to suggest a scenario whereby all of these people were in a room together (OK, big room I know) and into that room came a clown with a water pistol shouting *"My old man's a dustman"* squirting red liquid at everyone — out of all of the thoughts of what was occurring (and subsequent feelings of fear, terror or amusement), which one would be closest to reality? No two people in that vast room of the entire world's population would be having the exact same experience of the event. For starters, everyone would be at a slightly different vantage point. There's also everyone's own historical experience filtering everything that's occurring to consider. Some might think that clowns are spooky and some might think of them as funny. I personally find them a bit spooky, but have you seen Stephen King's *'It'*?

Everyone will be in a slightly different mood and have different levels of awareness at the time. There will essentially be seven billion differing levels of consciousness and seven billion different realities in the room.

This is where it gets really interesting, because if none of the realities are the one and only true reality, where is reality being created? Answer: it *has to be* created from within, no exceptions. It's all self-created. <u>Reality is only ever what you make it for yourself.</u> Everyone can have an infinite number or variety of thought responses to an external circumstance, which one it is depends entirely on the *person thinking it and not the circumstance.* Every reality is created from the inside-out and recognising the connection between thought and behaviour enables us to see where behaviour originates, which is in thought – every time. Go and ask 1000 rich people if they're happy. Do you think you'll get 1000 *"Yes"* responses? There are no outside-in rules for happiness. Unhappy lottery winners remain unhappy. Happy lottery winners remain happy. Every single person on the planet creates their own reality from the inside-out. That is just how it works.

Now I'm not saying that nothing in the outside world exists. I'm saying that nothing in the outside world exists <u>for us</u>, unless we create it from the inside-out <u>through thought</u>. Life is, after all, a contact sport. People get ill and die... bad stuff happens. It's just that the reality we create for ourselves based upon the stuff that does happen is entirely created by us. We get to make it up as we go along! Although it looks like the circumstances are the creator of our feelings, it's only ever <u>us</u> doing the creating, via thought.

When I start to talk about this in the training that I do, I get quite a few people saying *"I get that, but what about our subconscious thoughts, we surely don't have any control over those?"* OK, well firstly, I am not talking about controlling anything. You go off down that route and you'll get yourself into trouble. What I am talking about here is 'before the form' and by that I mean: it's not about what's being created, it's about what's doing the creating (K. Blevens 2012). As Syd Banks said: *"It's not about <u>what</u> you think, it's the fact <u>that</u> you think"*.

The process that creates our realities in every single human being on the planet is the same one. Mind, Thought and Consciousness (or whatever you wish to call them) are doing the creating for everyone. There are no exceptions. The process is always the same before the form, but what comes out of that process is different for every single one of us. This is why, when we start to look at what is being created, we're onto a hiding to nothing. Psychology and psychiatry could spend the rest of the days of creation looking at that stuff because there's an infinite supply of it! Every single one of us produces different thoughts to the next person in any given moment. Thoughts are like snowflakes in that respect: no two are alike. So why do we think that we could ever try and figure out what's going on when we start to analyse each individual thought? It would take forever! However, by looking at what is *doing* the creating, we get to see the bigger picture. We can see how the engine room of thought works, so that no matter what is being produced, we at least know what is going on behind the scenes. Then we don't have to attach anything to it, because we know that is only ever *us* doing the attaching in the first place. We don't have to do anything at all. That's right... do nothing!

A really good example of this is if I start to talk about something that you hear, which starts to 'make' you feel uncomfortable. Let's say that you are afraid of spiders and I start to describe the creepy little hairy poisonous, sneaky monsters who crawl up and down your bed at night looking for victims. Now, if you were picturing what I said in your head, no doubt you would be getting some feelings as a result. You then turn to me and say *"But if you hadn't told me that, I would not have felt it, therefore it MUST have been you causing those feelings because before I was fine, and now I'm not!"* Now imagine at the same time, there was someone else in the room hearing the exact same words as you who happens to be a spider expert. Those words were having a completely different effect on him. OK, so we now *know* it's not the words themselves that caused the feeling. If it was, then everyone would be feeling the same. So what is it then? The next option is to look to me as the culprit, but again, the other person did not get the same feelings, so it can't be me!

What is the missing link in this chain? Thought! It is only because we look at the above scenario and the feeling we get is instantaneous, that we naturally ascribe the blame to the person who delivered it. We 'shoot the messenger'! *"It wasn't there before, but it is now – cause and effect!"* we say. But t his is an illusion! We have created this feeling ourselves from the inside out. It just *looks like* it came from the outside it.

Having an understanding of this means that the infinite number of responses to the above scenario are all now 'still on'. The one we assigned to it no longer holds water, so we can now experience any of the others. How liberating is that? So when white van man cuts you up on the road, if you understand what is *actually* happening, not what *looks like* is happening, you have the freedom to see the situation (and respond) in infinite ways, <u>not just one!</u>

Now with specific regard to the subconscious, I believe that it is merely a description of thoughts that we are not aware of. We still can't have an experience of anything unless it comes via thought. If we could, that would be like saying there is some invisible force that controls us. There are certainly thoughts that are not as visible as others. I will be going into these later on in the book (such as the 'as if' thoughts in the Relationship chapter). Whatever we call them though, they are *still* thought. At some stage in our lives, something has happened and we have given our own meaning to it, based on what we know at the time. So if you were bitten by a dog when you were a child and you have ascribed a meaning to that event, such as all dogs are dangerous, it is still *you* doing the attaching here. We may have thoughts about this that are not obvious. Whenever we are in a situation that involves dogs, we may not be consciously aware that we are thinking about a past event, but those thoughts are still there giving us the feelings of unease. Is that unease real? Well it is certainly real for us because we are feeling it. Will it mean that we will be getting bitten by the dog? Probably not. Do you see the difference? We are creating the reality for ourselves, despite what is actually happening. We are the ones making it up!

So what has this got to do with *doing nothing?* Well, as I've already touched upon, the degree to which we freak ourselves out is the degree to which we splash around in our own thoughts, conscious or subconscious. Think about the last time you had an argument with your spouse. Think about how you were feeling when it happened. Do you remember the rush of thoughts in your head about the situation at the time? Then how did you feel a few hours later – any different?

I know that for me, when it's all 'kicking off', my thinking goes totally hay-wire. I start to have all sorts of wayward thoughts about the other person doing it to me intentionally – they're out to get me, big time! I might also be having a few subconscious thoughts about being hurt by someone that I love. Whether I am aware of them or not, the feelings I get at the time are entirely down to my own creation, via my thinking. How do I know this? Because a few hours later all my feelings of unease have dissipated. My thinking has calmed down and I am able to look at the situation with fresh eyes and a renewed sense of inner peace. So what happened there then?

Well, like the waves on the ocean, fresh thought always replaces the old ones. Like a glass of water with the sediment stirred up, if you leave it alone for a while, the sediment settles and the water clears. So it is with our thinking – when it gets stirred up a bit, you'll have trouble seeing anything clearly. Let it be and it'll return to a default position of calm. Now how do you think doing nothing would sit within this little scenario?

I'm certainly not saying that it's easy at first. When those feelings of unrest rise up in your belly, it feels like the last thing you should be doing is nothing. But those feelings are actually a warning signal from the brain. We take them to mean 'act now', when in fact they are actually telling us to 'proceed with caution' or 'back-off' from the situation until we can see things more clearly. So many times I have chosen to ignore this and ended up regretting it!

When we see that this is how the system works, we can let it do so without interfering or trying to change it. That's where we go wrong so often, trying to *change* our thoughts – or what is being created. We see the end product and we don't like it, so we try to change the whole system. That would be like buying a new car every time we get dirt on the current one! But the beauty of life and being human is that we do get to change. One day we have happy thoughts and the next we have sad ones. We think that it is the thoughts that need to change, so we go and try to change them (be positive!) But the ever changing nature of life is just that, ever changing. By letting nature takes it's course, we get to experience all kinds of thoughts and feelings. In fact, without experiencing unhappy thoughts we might not appreciate the happy ones. So they are all valuable to us, whether we think they are or not.

In addition to this understanding of how the system works, beyond our limited personal thought systems lies a vast reservoir of wisdom, insight and spiritual intelligence. Have you ever had an intuitive feeling or thought that turned out to be bang on the money, despite all the facts pointing in the other direction? If you ask anyone where their 'A-ha' moments come from, where the problem solving solutions arise or when they have their best ideas, you will start to see a trend.

A recent survey asked senior executives this very question and the responses were strikingly similar: *"In the shower"*, *"Whilst shaving"*, *"On holiday"*, *"Playing golf"*, *"On a run"*, *"Taking the dog for a walk"*. This is simply because, whenever the thinking clears, new insights emerge.

I've had seemingly impossible problems to deal with in the past, but now that I understand how the process works, I just go ahead and do nothing! I stop thinking about it and go for a long walk instead (OK, so a walk isn't nothing, but I'm talking about thought here). As I'm strolling through the woods near my house I'll get especially taken in by the beautiful colours in the trees. I'll take deep breaths of the crisp clean air and start thinking about all the animals burrowing underground and how they seem to know what to do and when to do it, without the need for any instruction manual. In short, I'm not thinking about the situation that had me thinking before the walk and that's when it usually hits me. The answer is sometimes so simple it's almost crazy that I hadn't seen it before. I had had, in my head one understanding of the situation – it wasn't necessarily the right one and it certainly wasn't clear. But when my thinking settles, I regain clarity.

A nice little story to illustrate this was when I lived in Spain for a year to learn Spanish. My flat mate and I met up with a Dutch couple who were very much into partying. They were also there to learn the language, so on occasions we used to try to just talk in Spanish. It never lasted long but at least we tried. I remember one particular evening, we had a long dinner and spent the rest of the evening soaking up the culture (and Rioja) in the bars of Madrid. David (strange name for a Dutchman, I know) and I had been talking outside one of the bars when it suddenly hit us. For the past hour at least, we had been talking entirely in Spanish. We hadn't even realised it up until that point. It was as if we had both been in some kind of trance. In actual fact, we had stopped thinking about it. We let go of our inhibitions of our lack of ability to do something that we could actually do, but thought we couldn't. We were essentially doing nothing!

Sometimes I just sit with nothing on my mind and the same result occurs. My point is that I simply *let it go*, and the answer emerges. It just comes from a different level of thought than that which created it, yet it seems so obvious. Because 'A-ha' moments are most likely to come when there is nothing on our minds. We simply cannot force an insight.

This is not to say that you may not get an insight when there is plenty on your mind. I know many people who can testify to this. In fact, they have told me that they have had insights when they were feeling down right depressed or insanely busy, when suddenly an insight popped up and they had a realisation of huge magnitude.

The important fact is that the insight just came, it wasn't forced in any way. How often has this happened to you, when an answer came from (seemingly) nowhere to a problem that needed solving? No one person has greater access to wisdom than any other person. Mental health is the resting state, or default setting of the mind. Remember the children in the playground?

Here's another example perfectly illustrated by Jack Pransky in *Somebody Should Have Told Us!*: If I hold a gun to your head and say *"Give me your money or your life!"* some people would say *"Money"* and some people would say *"Life"*. What is it about the situation that has changed? Nothing. It is your own *choice* that decides your fate. I would suggest that at the very moment that the gun was pointed to your head, you would want a clear mind to decide what to choose. In fact people who have had this very situation happen to them report just that, a moment of total clarity. They absolutely knew what to do and which option to choose!

So essentially what I am going to talk about in the coming chapters is how this understanding, that we are more than just our thoughts, can be applied to everyday life. I will explain how it is often so much better to simply *do nothing!* and get the answers we need (via our own innate wisdom) to live a much better life. If you're dealing with day-to-day circumstances that require clear thinking, it's better to have less on your mind, don't you think? Worrying about stuff is just using up mental bandwidth. It's not practical. It's not even necessary. So why do we do it? Because we don't understand how the system works, that's why. These Principles are like a mental handbook. They explain *how your mind actually works*. When life deals up the bad stuff (as it will), like illness and death and job losses and accidents and selfish friends and... whatever, don't you think that being able to deal with it from a place of clarity and wisdom would be a better option than wasting hours of your life worrying about it?

I used to get so down and low about stuff that I would try to alleviate my suffering with all sorts of nonsense: drugs, alcohol, sex, shopping, anything that I *thought* would take the bad feelings away. Little did I know that there was nothing that I actually needed to do. If only I had realised that I was the one creating the feelings via my thoughts; that I was the one making it all up in the first place! I was getting fooled by the illusion that what was out there was causing what was going on inside of me.

When you see yourself getting fooled by this illusion: that every day circumstances are causing your bad feelings, if you simply realise it and do nothing about it, your mind will eventually return to default – like the disturbed sediment in a glass of water will settle when left alone and clarity returns.

Now this is just the tip of a very large, Titanic sinking iceberg. In Syd's own words, "*Even people locked up in mental institutions are sitting in the middle of mental health and they don't even know it.*" How can this be true when one after another medical professional has written them off? When we see that our realities are being created moment to moment by our thinking, but we know that there is an underlying source of wisdom at our disposal, we can tap into it without doing anything.

"*Oh, if only it wasn't so very simple... how much easier it would be to comprehend!*" But wait, it gets better, because the next question to ask is: well who or what is creating this in the first place? I'm going to be addressing this bit in the second part of this chapter later on.

In the meantime though, I'm going to keep referring back to these Principles throughout. By now, you might well be thinking "*There's something in that, but I'm not sure what it is*". That's good! Being puzzled is good. It means that your intellect has given up a bit of space and your intuition is having a say – and we all know where that intuition comes from, don't we?

We all know that you can 'get' something intellectually and you can 'know' something to be real. Big difference. We're talking about the latter here. It's not something that is obvious (or we'd all be doing it), if anything it seems totally counter-intuitive, but the understanding is already within you, which is why you might be reading this now and feeling a sense that there <u>is</u> something to it. That is because you already have it, it's just been obscured by years of thought. <u>These Principles, that are the gift with which you create your own reality, are the same Principles that have created the illusion of thought that you are separate from it</u>. But you are not separate! You have never been separate.

What if everyone on the planet had this basic knowledge and 'knew' that their feelings <u>weren't</u> coming from the other person, but were being made up by themselves? Do you think there would be any more wars? Because people would start to see the innocence of their own frustrations and anger and would take things less personally.

In the meantime however, let's stick with you. Let's see what an understanding of the Principles can do for you and your Relationships.

Chapter Three

Relationships

Morpheus: "There is a difference between knowing the path and walking the path."

Right, so let's start with an easy one, shall we...?! I'm not going to beat around the bush here. There are things I am about to say which fly in the face of pretty much every bit of advice you may already have heard with regard to relationships (and there's been a lot!) However, what I am about to tell you is not 'advice' as such. Nothing in this book can be described as advice really, because it is simply an understanding of how the system works. What you do with it is completely up to you.

Unfortunately, I came to this understanding too late to save my marriage but that's what fate has in store for us sometimes. I am now deeply blessed to be with my life-long spiritual partner. We found each other, funnily enough by doing nothing! In fact, it was pretty much to the second that I had decided that I was not ready for another relationship (having just been on my third date after the divorce) that it happened. I stopped trying and surrendered and Victoria came into my life. But enough about me, let's dive in.

Syd Banks, when he talked about relationships, suggested that positivity and understanding were the keys to a successful relationship. Through happiness, the problems of the relationship would take care of themselves. OK, so this is probably not something you won't have heard of before but let's explore a little further shall we?

Now this is all well and good (I hear you say) when things are going swimmingly, but what about when the going gets tough? Yes, well it certainly looks like things need sorting out when that happens, but let me ask you this: remember the last time you had an email from someone at work (or a friend or family member) that you got really cross about? You know, the one where you started to reply to them *at that moment*... but then chose not to send it? Yes, that one! When you re-read the rant that you were about to send later on with a calm head, how did you feel about it? Chances are that it made you squirm or you said "*Oh my God, I am so glad I did not send that!*" Yet, in the moment, you were bang on the money, absolutely sure, beyond a shadow of a doubt that you were right (and within your rights) to reply to them in that manner. So why on earth do we think that we are in a position, when we are in a heated argument with our spouse about anything that we think is 'making' us angry, to be able to sort it out – *at that moment?* It happens every time and every time we regret what we said afterwards or think, 'why didn't I just walk away and talk about it later?'

I remember Dr George Pransky (who is an expert in this particular field) telling a group at a seminar that he and his wife, Linda had a row once when they were travelling. They were both very tired and drained and at that particular moment when the row began, they could both have been hooked up to a lie detector machine and it would have absolutely, positively given a full-on 100%: "*Yup, they're tellin' the truth right now*" reading. So what did they say at that very moment in time? George: "*You know, marrying you was the single biggest mistake I have ever made in my entire life*". Linda:

"You're right, I agree".

Fortunately, Linda then turned to George and said: "You know, George, if we didn't know what we do know, that could have been bad". And that was it. The sting had been taken out of the argument and it was over, because what they both knew, and I will share with you shortly, is that the primary reason that arguments occur in the first place is our basic misunderstanding of a very simple concept.

First though, I want to address the subject of moods. Moods are also just thought, but when we are in a low mood we receive faulty information from the brain and if we take that information and believe it or trust it, things can take a turn for the worse. If I had a pound for every time this had happened to me, or I had seen it happen to someone else, I would have enough money to pay off the national debt!

In my previous relationship when my ex-wife and I used to argue, I would often ask that we wait until I was in a better frame of mind to sort things out (if I was feeling low). She, however, would want to get to the bottom of the situation right there and then, no matter how we were both feeling, so we were already in dangerous territory. The information I was receiving to my brain was often way off the mark as a consequence: 'She's only doing this to get at me', 'Why does she always bring this up?'. My brain was telling me that it was *her* that was the reason that I was feeling bad and I was falling for it hook, line and sinker!

We swear blind that it is the circumstances or the words of the other person that are causing the feelings of our resentment; that these words somehow have a life of their own, like some kind of transmutable virus that you can catch by being exposed to them – *"But it only started to happen once she said it, so it must be her!"*

This is actually the part where we are getting fooled. You see, we're missing out one very vital step in the process... thought.

Don't forget, <u>we can't have an experience about anything unless we have a thought about it</u>, and that includes whatever abuse your wife just hurled at you. Some days it may seem worse that others: same words, different feeling – different thoughts. Because thoughts are changing all the time. In fact, it is absolutely impossible to hold on to a thought for more than a few seconds. Go on, try it now. See if you can hold onto a thought for longer than a few seconds. It's impossible. Think of your favourite holiday destination and try to keep thinking about it for the next five minutes: nothing else, just that.

Still thinking about it? No, thought not. Or if you think you did, let me know if there were any other thoughts at all that surfaced during that time (yes, the one telling you that you are still thinking about it was another thought). Our thoughts are like the clouds drifting through the sky. It's raining today, but it'll be sunny tomorrow! <u>Another thought will always come along in a moment</u>. It's the ever changing world of our thinking. It just 'is'.

Having the knowledge that our thoughts are all self-created using the Three Principles of Mind, Thought and Consciousness and knowing that another thought will be along shortly is very liberating. Instead of being dragged down into the spiral of negative thoughts and feelings, one is able to simply see what is going on and do nothing! It's not even about the doing, it's *all* about the understanding. Remember the tide analogy? Just knowing this is how it works, is the key here.

So the best way then to deal with someone in a low mood is to be understanding and to overlook their behaviour *at that moment*.

If you see that it is the thoughts that create the distress, you'll see that moods are just thought, they aren't real and won't last forever! Our thinking and our moods will always fluctuate – it's the very nature of thought (and life) itself. Whatever we *feel* is down to how we are *thinking* at that given moment.

So what is the primary reason that any argument happens in the first place? It is a basic misunderstanding of this process, nicely summed up in the following sentence: *We are always feeling our thinking!* Now this is a very important point to grasp fully. <u>We cannot have an experience of anything unless we have a thought about it</u>. I know it *looks like* we bypass the thought process sometimes because the feeling is so instantaneous, but it only ever comes to us *via thought*. It looks like we are having an experience about the 'thing', when in fact we are only having an experience about our thinking, about the thing. Does that make sense? If it doesn't, keep having a look through the previous paragraphs until it clicks. All feelings, whether good or bad <u>must</u> come via thought.

There is a condition called Congenital Analgesia which arises due to a mutation in the SCN9A gene which causes misfiring brain signals. Children who have this condition do not sense physical pain coming in from outside stimuli. They often break bones, lose teeth, get cuts, bruises and bites (in their own mouths) without the body even knowing about it, which can be potentially dangerous – for obvious reasons. The lack of thought to tell them there is a problem is the key here. As far as they are concerned, there is nothing wrong.

Thought precedes feeling, every time – without exception. Who makes up the thoughts? You do. When we get fooled by believing that it is our circumstances that are causing our thinking (rather than us making it up), we dive head first into an argument *about the circumstances.* Sound familiar? If we can see that it is our own reaction to it that is the issue here and not the circumstance itself, then we have a better chance of dealing with the situation with compassion and understanding.

OK, so I like to give examples wherever I can, and there is a perfect little story to illustrate this point that happened to me only recently. My lovely partner Victoria was flying to Ecuador on a business trip. She had booked first class and was looking forward to getting to the airport and relaxing in the VIP lounge before take-off. It was an early flight, so at 6am in the morning and a little jaded, we walked up to the first class queue at Continental Airlines. The security lady checked Victoria's passport and informed her that she needed an ESTA (Electronic System for Travel Authorisation) visa for her transfer from the US to Ecuador. Victoria, in an early morning low state of mind, took a dislike to the whole situation, having spent a lot of money on the flight and not having been informed of this requirement prior to arrival. It was no doubt on the booking page somewhere but she had overlooked it. The lady told us that we needed to go down to the internet cafe and fill in the forms ourselves. Not being in the best frame of mind to start with, this really got her goat. Yet, as I was listening to her protestations, I realised that her low mood state was a large contributing factor to the situation and to her own annoyance. She was being totally fooled by her own thinking and innocently ascribing the feelings of annoyance to the circumstances. What was the best thing for me to do? Well, I agreed with her compassionately and suggested we do as the lady said and get it sorted. I was not in the best mood either might I add, but I recognised that getting stuck into the negative thinking (or the officious lady for that matter) was really not the best policy.

A couple of days later when Victoria called me from her hacienda in Ecuador, she explained what had happened. *"You know, what was really bugging me, but I didn't realise it until afterwards, was that I just wanted to spend as much time with you before I left and that I was really going to miss you".* Now I certainly didn't see *that* at the time and any amount of discussion in the moment would not have unearthed that little gem. But by being compassionate and understanding, I was able to let Victoria's mood naturally rise again with no damage done. She worked out the real reason in her own time.

I hope that gives you a good illustration of what can happen when you are able to see yourself getting caught up in the illusion. It happens on a daily basis to everyone, only with this understanding you get to see what is happening sooner than before — you get to actually *see yourself making it up* as you go along. When feelings of hurt or anxiety take over in your belly, you get to see that you have created these too, via your thinking.

It can get quite comical at times, as you start to descend into the negative spiral and the thoughts are coming at you thick and fast about how terrible this and that is... and then you stop. You realise what is happening, see the trick being done and do nothing! Rather than have to go through the shouting and yelling; then the self realisation that you over-reacted; followed by the apologies, back-tracking and flower buying — instead you can be in the moment with compassion and love. It's so liberating and it'll save you a whole heap of cash on flower bills!

Compatibility

OK, that's the basics on thought, feeling and moods covered. Now let's use your new level of understanding and apply it to some other everyday relationship 'problems'.

I mentioned previously that Dr George Pransky was, and still is, one of the leading authorities on this subject. Some of what I am about to share with you has been taken from his excellent book called 'The Relationship Handbook'. I recommend this book highly, so please do get a copy when you can. Right, let's get stuck in...

Complimentary and incompatible are two sides of the same coin depending on how one 'thinks' about it. What seems like a refreshing difference one day, can seem like a pain in the backside the next. What's the difference that makes the difference? Yup, it's that pesky thought again, which as you may now know by now, is actually created by you! Childish can seem childlike, opinionated can seem outspoken, unrealistic can seem optimistic – you get the idea. Because when the emotional connection is there in your thinking, all of the differences pale into insignificance.

There are many, many examples of successful marriages that have worked against all the odds. Such a hotchpotch of unlikely, seemingly incompatible couples who do fine, thanks for asking. Look at some of the people that you know or some of the celebrity marriages that have stood the test of time. True compatibility is sharing a positive feeling, which comes from thought. It is enjoying each other's company, no matter what the differences are. Closeness brings out the best in a relationship... it is binding and altogether inspiring.

OK, so let's illustrate this with an example: Michael and Davina have been married for five years. Michael wants kids, Davina doesn't.

During discussions with them regarding their incompatibility, they both realised that the times that they were not thinking about children, they got on great. When either of them was feeling insecure, the thoughts about the incompatibility seemed to get worse. They realised that the more energy they were putting into the thinking about children, the less they were enjoying the relationship itself. So their homework for two weeks after seeing George, was to do nothing! With specific regard to the child issue anyway. They were told to put 'that one' on the back-burner and go and simply enjoy their time together. Just value and cherish each other for what they liked about one another and not think about anything else <u>but</u> this.

Two weeks later, they returned. By not thinking about the issue, but focussing on how positive they were about each other, they felt relieved. They both felt like they had done just after they were first married. The issue wasn't any more resolved, it just didn't bother them so much. Interestingly enough, Davina later realised that her reluctance to have children was based on a belief that Michael would not take enough responsibility for the child care and that she would be left literally 'holding the baby'. Michael realised that his own desire to have children was based around his own insecurities. He had mellowed on the idea and Davina had grown into it. How interesting! Because they *did nothing* on the issue itself, putting it on the back-burner, their own inner wisdom was able to unravel some of the underlying reasons behind the problem. They discovered a new understanding about themselves, each other and the situation, purely by doing nothing!

Now I'm not saying that in all cases, the best way forward is to just accept that bliss can be fully restored by this approach. There will sometimes be a genuine feeling of ill-ease in a relationship. This could be your own inner wisdom trying to tell you something important. Just try not to let your *thinking* cloud your judgement. Your own inner wisdom has a knack of getting things right after all!

Victoria was only asking me the other day about when to trust the feeling. She had been in a job in the City for seven years and had always felt that it had been wrong. It led her to suffer from years of depression. I would say that her body and mind was giving her some pretty surefire signals that something was up there.

So listen to your wisdom on this one. If it feels right, it probably is – and if it doesn't...

Communication

Communication is quite simply the pipe through which the feelings in your relationship travel. If you are experiencing bad feelings, then it would be better if communication wasn't used at all! A flippant remark, but it makes sense doesn't it? If you could communicate your ill-feelings across to the other person more effectively, would that make things better?

It is the quality of the feelings that pass through the pipe, the communication channel, that makes the difference. So if you are angry and you communicate anger, communication is not the problem. Angry thoughts create angry feelings. Period!

So what if a couple simply cannot communicate with each other without feeling upset? They start out with a preconception that 'this will not go well'. Essentially, they are communicating perfectly, because it enables them to share their bad feelings that they're focusing on. Communication is neutral, it simply carries the feelings being conveyed. <u>Communication isn't nearly as important</u>

as how we feel when we're doing it!

Simply understand that when you're feeling low, it's probably a good idea not to talk about things unless you can *see* that you're doing the creating yourself, and not the other person. This is where we get into trouble. We have the feelings of hurt, pain or anxiety and we ascribe the *cause* of the feeling to the other person. Then we try to talk about things *as if they were the ones responsible!* Can you see how this makes no sense at all, if you are the one who is doing the creating of all of your feelings in the first place?

Now, remember what I said earlier about not taking what we are thinking seriously if we are in a low mood – our brain is giving us faulty signals not to be trusted (the chemistry in our brain actually changes when we are having an argument). However, our moods (which are still just thoughts) are part of a natural cycle – some days we just feel better than others. Have you ever noticed that if you have a conversation with your spouse on a day when things are looking rosy, especially about something that is usually confrontational, things happen differently? When my ex-wife and I talked about a divorce, there was a huge difference in the conversations that were had in a bad mood (threats, shouting) and the ones had in a good mood (hopeful outlook, better for the kids in the long run).

That's not to say that you can't talk about things when you're in a low mood. If you can see that you're doing the creating and you're fully aware that any feelings of angst are being generated *by you and not by them* from moment to moment, then please continue. I know that for me now, if I find myself 'heading south', but I see that I am doing this through my own thinking, I am able to pull out of the tail-spin a whole lot quicker. I still prefer to have any difficult discussions when I am feeling calm and relaxed and can see things clearly – but that's just my own personal preference.

Intimacy

If you think that intimacy requires a large investment of time and energy, think again. When couples don't know where intimacy comes from they have to exert a large amount of energy to get it back. But intimacy is actually very simple. It's easier than we think to obtain and requires very little effort – *because it never went anywhere in the first place!* It's just our thinking about intimacy that changed (I hope you're starting to see a common thread here).

OK, so let's imagine a couple who are not as intimate as they were before. They go for a meal and are sitting across the table from each other. (She says to him:) *"Why aren't we as close as we used to be, I want to feel close to you"*. *"We are close, I mean I booked this table, we're spending time together now, aren't we?"* (sound familiar?) *"No, I mean really close"*. *"Look, I've got a lot on my mind at the moment, what with the problems at work and our son going to university"*.

Might I suggest that there is a clue in there somewhere? Intimacy is actually a natural state. It's what happens when two people are together with *nothing on their minds*. Closeness does not require much time or effort. In fact it requires a fair bit of doing nothing! Couples who try to achieve closeness are putting way too much *thought* into it. They might mistakenly see the clearing of the air after a fight as a means to achieve it, so they try this approach again and again, recreating what they think is the way to attain it. But these fights are unnecessary, because intimacy can also be achieved when both partners are totally present with each other.

Using 'busyness' as an excuse doesn't wash either. As long as both of you are totally present with each other, then intimacy prevails. It's not children, shopping, business meetings, mothers-in-law, money problems (etc) that are causing the problems, it's merely the thoughts about them. Once you realise that these distractions are extraneous and you are present in the moment, closeness will come naturally.

In short, if you want to get your intimacy back, just *be* with your partner with nothing on your mind... Mentally: do nothing! I'll leave the physical bits up to you!

Commitment

Ooh, good one. Let's see what we can do with this, shall we?

When you choose to focus on a task and become totally committed to it, what happens? Does the task seem to flow more, does it seem easier, does time seem to go faster? Conversely, when you're unsure of something, how does that feel? Does time slow down, do you get bogged down in thought about what you should be doing instead? When this applies to a partner, how does that feel? If you choose to focus on someone and really 'be' with them, what happens? Might I suggest that you go back to the previous section and get the answer to that one...?! But what about those nagging doubts in the back of your mind, maybe in the early days of a relationship? What's all that about then?

OK, so let's imagine that Dave and Angie have been going out for a few months and Angie is starting to fall for Dave. But Dave has been watching a few too many music videos and thinks that Angie is not glamorous enough for him. What's going on here?

Well, firstly, Dave has set himself some specific requirements for his own happiness. He is being fooled by thinking that something from the outside-in will *make* him happy. He is also losing track of the things that he likes about Angie, because his own insecurities (a woman must look a certain way to make me happy) are taking pole position. Honestly, the media has a lot to answer for in my opinion!

I don't know about you, but I have had friends who have dated models and in every case bar one, it's only lasted a short time. Why? Because they realised that the look was the main thing that was attracting them, they were being fooled from the outside-in. As they went to a deeper, human level, there was little or no connection. It's like when you buy a new car. It's great fun for a while, you treat it like it's crystal glass on four wheels, but the feeling doesn't last forever. Eventually it gets dirty and you're not so bothered if you get a scratch or two.

Anyway, back to our human analogy. Angie can sense that something is up. Their time together seems to be less fun than it was and Dave seems distracted more often than not. They both start justifying their feelings against their thoughts, entering a downward spiral of incompatibility. Further thoughts of justification follow and break-up soon occurs. Now, what if Dave realised the effect that his lack of commitment and looking elsewhere was having on the possibility of having a great relationship with Angie? What if he could actually see that he is focussing on his *own insecurities* rather than the reality of who Angie actually is? If only he could see that his own thinking is souring his perspective and compromising his experience of being with her fully in the moment. Let's say that Angie is a really special lady who has an inkling for this understanding. She likes Dave a lot, and she realises that his insecurities are all that is getting in the way of them having a great time together. She feels compassion for Dave and she's not going to take his insecurities personally. Angie's calm certainty and understanding stops Dave in his tracks. Dave starts to think more deeply about his own insecurities. He starts to notice how superficial his thoughts are, how they are based on a preconception given to him by someone/thing else. He starts to notice Angie in a different way, how kind and loving she is and how much time she gives people with her attentiveness.

He starts to think about what he really wants and sees that Angie is a person for whom compassion and understanding are key. How much better would it be, to spend time with someone like that, who realises the true value of living life in the moment with passion, than with someone who takes it all for granted and lives from the outside-in?

He realises how commitment is not a sacrifice but is actually self fulfilling. Once you are fully involved, you get so much more out of it. So Dave lets his previous thinking go and becomes more present with Angie – he commits. The time he spends with her is more meaningful and much deeper. He begins to really see himself and her together and eventually they fall in love. Could this happen? Well, this is a true story, so I guess it already has (names changed... but you know who you are).

The thing is, if you are consumed by problems and fearful thoughts, you're too preoccupied to notice or enjoy what's going on around you. <u>Negative thoughts contaminate relationships and insecure thoughts pull the reins back on intimacy.</u> By having an understanding of how your thinking is created, you are less likely to indulge in insecure thoughts that keep you from enjoying your relationship. You get to see these thoughts as just clouds in the sky, and not the sky itself.

When we're young, we get all sorts of thinking from our parents and siblings which we put energy into. *"Don't trust people with their eyes too close together"*, *"Make sure you find a man with means"*, *"He's got to make you laugh or it won't last..."*. You get the idea. The thing is, those thoughts are just thoughts. You have assigned meaning to them yourself. You've chosen to put energy into them and make them real for you. Does it mean they aren't true? Who knows? The fact is though, that they are still *just thoughts*. It would be better to trust your own judgment, intuition and inner wisdom (as Dave ended up doing), than to be a slave to thinking that is only a reality because you made it so, and isn't even your own to begin with! (It's not surprising really, we take what our parents say very seriously when we are children. I'll be delving deeper into this in the chapter on Parenting later on in the book.)

He cheated on me...!

OK, now I've put a cat amongst the pigeons! How are we going to deal with this one then? Well... anger and resentment are painful feelings, that's for sure. But where do feelings come from? That's right, it's thought. If you have a thorn in your foot, do you keep walking around with it digging in, or do you take it out? Self inflicted emotional pain is like walking around whilst keeping the thorn firmly embedded in the foot.

It's true, that when there is a big issue like infidelity, the negative thinking about it overshadows the feelings of love, which darkens the outlook and sends both partners into a downward spiral. The couple gets discouraged and want to call it a day. For the relationship to work, the spiral must be reversed (or ideally not entered into in the first place), which means addressing the thinking. Forgiving and forgetting are the important ingredients here. The infidelity is still only being kept alive by thought. If this sounds like a 'cop out', just think about it – putting energy into a pool of painful memories in their minds, this couple are walking around with the splinter still in the foot. Once a memory is forgiven, it is more easily forgotten. To see this in action, take the example of a man whose wife cheated on him. He has just learned, however, that she has an incurable cancer and only has a few months to live – so he lets go of past resentments to care for her. If he can do it then, why can't he do it at will? Whatever the 'reason' he is telling himself, the fact is that *he can do it*. However you reason 'the thinking' at the end of the day, is up to you – but it's still <u>just</u> thought!

You see, forgiveness is a self serving act. If you are in pain, you suffer. Getting rid of the pain is actually a nice thing to do for yourself. You are taking the thorn out of the foot. <u>Forgiveness is an act of seeing your painful thoughts with 'understanding'</u>. This means seeing the humanity of others, not taking it personally and seeing it as just, *part of life*. Do you see what I'm getting at here? Remember: we are only feeling our thinking *about the circumstance*, not the circumstance itself.

Recently, there has been a spate of knife crime in London, and as a result, a number of teenagers have lost their lives in gang related murders. Most of the pictures and footage on the news focuses on the angry parents of the victims, but occasionally you will see parents at peace. Parents who have chosen to forgive the perpetrator of the crime. They realise that their son's murderer was only doing what they thought was best for them at that time, based on what they knew and what they were thinking. People tend to act out of insecurity when they engage in counterproductive behaviour and the more misguided, the greater the insecurity! The parents who saw this in their son's murderer, therefore found compassion for them instead of hatred.

Within a relationship, assuming that it was a strong one (and not just a one night stand), if one partner cheats, the reason for doing so is likely to be firmly embedded within this feeling of insecurity. To get a couple who has trust issues back on the right track, the first way to do it (assuming that they don't already have an understanding of where their thoughts are coming from) is to raise their level of *feeling* towards each other. How? Help them to understand what is being created (feeling via thought) and who is doing the creating. People prefer to feel kindness rather than malice towards their partner, so they will start to see that the painful thoughts are actually getting in the way of a peaceful, happy life. Next, encourage them to see the innocence in the other person's actions – because through understanding will come the healing.

"But what if I can't forgive him/her?" Some people have the mistaken idea that holding resentments somehow protects them from making the same mistake again. That's like walking backwards down a street, looking at all the potholes you've fallen into. Surely you want to know where you're going... in the right direction!

"But if I do forgive him/her, am I not condoning their behaviour?" You have to learn to take what happened less personally. When people are unhappy, they do things that they wouldn't normally do: drink, gamble, work compulsively, feel sorry for themselves, overeat, shop till they're broke, have affairs. It is more to do with

their state of mind (which is their thinking) and how they react to and deal with their insecurity, than it is a reflection on you. Trust and security comes from understanding, and closeness comes from trust and security. It's certainly easier to access your wisdom with a clear head, which is where forgiving and forgetting come in.

Once again, if your inner wisdom is telling you something else here... trust it. If it's saying *"Look, I know why he/she did it, they've got a tonne of insecurity that they're trying to drown out. I get where it's coming from but I really think this person is not right for me. They're going to take a lot of effort to understand and get through this themselves and I'm not willing to commit that much time and effort (and love) to do it for them."* Well that's fine, you know what you need to do, but doing it from this place of higher awareness is better than the knee jerk reaction of 'he cheated, it's over', don't you think...?

Wrapping it all up

If we understand where the feelings are coming from in our relationships we are less likely to make the other person 'wrong' or take things personally and we will be more interested and curious as to how things *really* look for them.

Many people struggle with the notion of not taking things personally, because they feel that they have to defend themselves or they see it as backing down. When they see this is all created by thought, which is created by them from the inside-out and not by the other person, they are more likely to be in their wisdom. From this place of wisdom, they will see that taking it personally is unnecessary.

They can then actually get to help the other person to get back to their own wisdom more quickly by simply being in theirs – kind of like contagious compassion!

I hope you are getting the gist of what I am talking about here. I am not suggesting that you walk away from problems, rather simply be aware that when you have them, and want to talk about them or evaluate them for yourself, your *thinking* is <u>the</u> key variable. But whatever the circumstances, you won't find happiness in your unhappiness. Arguing and fighting with each other are simply counter-productive, especially when you can use your different standpoints as an opportunity to understand each other and the situation more deeply. Always try to listen deeply (with nothing on your mind) to the other person and see if there is another message behind their words – we'll be delving into this more in the Parenting chapter.

We all get fooled by the 'outside-in' world every day. Your new understanding of how thought works won't necessarily happen overnight, and there will be times when you get completely caught up in your thinking and don't see the situation for what it is. But having an understanding of these Principles and how the 'trick is done', lets you see yourself getting fooled *more quickly*. You get to spot your mind playing tricks on you more often.

Heaven knows, Victoria and I still have our moments, but we know what's happening now, so we don't take our thinking so seriously any more. It just gets us into trouble! Instead, we take a time out and let the thinking settle (like the sediment in the cloudy water) and look at it with fresh eyes and clear heads when it has.

If you *have* to do something, go and write an email and keep it as a draft to view later on – just to show you how your thinking went awry and how it's not wise to take knee-jerk action.

Just don't send it!

Relationships can be a great source for growth, they can evolve and deepen over time, so stick with it and make the most of them. Of course, when you are both feeling downright miserable — do nothing! Your brain is not working correctly and unless you can see exactly what's going on, you'll get yourself into trouble! Don't worry though, the clouds will pass and the sun will reappear eventually, as it always does.

Chapter Four

Business

Neo: "What are you trying to tell me? That I can dodge bullets?"
Morpheus: "No, Neo. I'm trying to tell you that when you're ready,
you won't have to."

That's all very well in relationships, (I hear you say) but what about in careers and business? This stuff is being taught to two star generals and four star admirals in the US military – they can't just do nothing! Well, actually, they can. At least, it would certainly be better for them if they responded to high pressure situations (ie war) from a place of wisdom and calm – rather than a reactive, angry state. Don't you think? Let's explore further.

There's been a lot of work done in this field with Fortune 500 and FTSE 100 companies in the US and UK. There are chief executives of some pretty major blue chips who have benefitted hugely from this understanding. Don't forget, we're talking about having the *understanding* here, not 'doing' anything, per se. Purely seeing how the system works is enough. One of the ways this is shown to them is via a variable called 'state of mind' (so not that different from moods really, but we are talking business speak here).

When they see the connection between what they are experiencing on a day-to-day basis and their state of mind; and the connection between state of mind and the Three Principles – they are then able to understand the whole process in a more meaningful and productive way.

They are able to understand where all of the results that they are seeing on a daily basis are *actually* coming from, and it's <u>not</u> from their circumstances (no matter how much it looks like it!) We are talking about an 'inside-out' approach here, don't forget – we create everything from the inside-out. 'Thought' is all generated from within, via the Principles. In business, it's easy for people to misinterpret company cultures and procedures for anything other than thought. But when you ask employees and really dig down into these, they will see that all of them originate and are held as a reality in the present by nothing other than thought.

It is however, sometimes harder to convince *business people* of this fact, than it is someone who has mental health issues. At a recent Three Principles conference in London, the psychiatrist Dr Bill Pettit brought everyone in the audience to tears by telling them: *"I know, for absolute certainty, that I can look into the eyes of every single person on this planet and tell them that they're going to be OK."* He had just described how he managed to get a manic psychotic named Molly out of her 'state', merely by discussing the Principles with her and telling her that she was actually perfectly healthy. Later, when Molly was able to talk properly again, she said that a little voice in her head had said: *"My God, they've sent me a psychiatrist crazier than I am"*, and then it told her *"But you know... he's right"*.

Later at the same conference, I bumped into Mara Gleason who works in the US with Fortune 500 companies teaching the Principles, and I said to her *"You know, when you hear Bill saying that, it makes our job of dealing with business people seem like peanuts doesn't it?"* She replied *"No, I think business is harder..."* We didn't have time to continue our discussion, but in the moments that followed I had my own insight into why she had said that.

If you are in a room full of twenty stressed out executives and you're showing them the example of the manic psychotic and telling them that their own circumstances are nothing to do with their own current state (of stress say) and here's a great example of this (referring to Molly), they'll tell you "*Well firstly, she was broken to start with... we're all healthy.*" And secondly, "*Are you trying to tell us that every single one of us, who can quite clearly see that these circumstances are making us stressed, are ALL wrong... that we're all delusional and making it up?*"

"*Yes, Sir. That's precisely what I am telling you...*"

Which leads us nicely onto our first section to tackle in business and it's a heart stopping biggie...

Stress

If you had asked someone in the 1600's about their health, they would probably have told you they accepted that they were most likely to die from the plague, or from a cut to the flesh, or from some other sort of unpleasant death (like being eaten by wolves or neighbours or something) that for most people at that time, was the 'norm' (OK, maybe not the neighbours bit).

Nowadays, we have a rather different outlook on our physical health, *apart* from when we look at stress. We see it as par for the course of our work life (and our lives in general). In fact, in business, if we're not stressed, we're not doing our jobs properly!

Let's agree on one thing here before we start – stress is NOT a good thing. If you are taking a winning putt in golf, or a three point match winning throw in basketball, or you're preparing a sales pitch or organising a wedding or preparing for a board meeting or even picking up the kids from school: if there is high tension and stress involved, it's not as good as if you are relaxed, focussed and calm. Period. Try doing anything in that state and it ain't gonna go smoothly!

Let's face it, people don't *like* to feel stressed. I know that some folk say that they work *better* with stress, but let's go for the other 99.9% of the world's population here shall we? So let's get to the bottom of it then and start with the following example:

If you take a plank of wood and place it on the floor and ask someone to walk across it, they will have no problem doing so (unless they have a plank phobia). But, if you raise that plank between two pillars, say 60ft in the air, their thinking now interferes... tension creeps in. But it's the SAME plank!

When Philippe Pettit, who walked on a tightrope between the Twin Towers in 1974, was asked about the risks involved, he said, *"To talk about risks is to miss the point. What interests me is the performance. It's the same tightrope I always use, to use it perfectly is the performance"*. It's only ever the *thinking* that makes the difference.

I know what you're going to say here, *"But the tightrope was suspended one hundred and ten stories high! Surely THAT makes a difference?"* Again, I know it looks like it, but it doesn't. It is still only the same tightrope and still only the *thinking* that makes it different. As soon as you attach your actions to an outcome or consequence, you've missed your opportunity for freedom — thinking changes and your involvement changes too. But that's only your thinking. You have 'done' the attaching yourself.

To demonstrate, let's go back to the inside-out idea and flip it. If we are saying that stress is created in any way, shape or form by the outside-in from circumstances, then we are assuming that there is stress out there already, waiting to be caught. We're saying that, just like catching a cold, we 'catch' stress. Not having enough resources, or time is the cause of the stress, so stay away from it, you might catch something! This of course, is absurd. Yet we feel it when it happens and it certainly *looks* real enough. The simple truth is, we always generate the stress in our own minds via thought. Always! As soon as we 'see' that we are creating this through our own thinking, we understand the process better and we can accept that our feelings are telling us that our thinking is skewed. Then we can assess the situation more accurately with better judgement, or wait until our thinking returns to normality (which it always will, if we let it).

When you see that these feelings are not coming from something that is outside of your own creation, that gives you a great deal of hope! You see that stress is really non existent! It's all self-created. All of it. Every feeling that you have is a result of a thought. Don't forget, thoughts are just energy that show up in your head. They move and shift like the waves on the sea. If you put unnecessary energy into them, you'll splash around in them making more waves. We don't have to *do* anything with them. Just knowing that this is how it works, we don't have to run away or stay and fight, there's nothing we have to do with them. Period!

When my ex-wife and I used to talk about money, I would get a stress ball in my stomach more often than not. Now that I know where this feeling was being is created, via my thinking (through the Principles), I look back on those conversations and I notice something very interesting. I didn't get those feelings on every occasion. Once in fact, I remember we were on holiday in Ireland

and having a wonderful time. We had a conversation about money that was reflective and hopeful. There was no argument, just acceptance, it was quite different. Of course, now I know why – we were both in a high quality of mind and things looked different. The situation was the same but it looked different in our thinking, so the feeling was also different.

OK, so now following on from that little analogy, I want you to try having a happy thought and a bad feeling, or a bad thought and a happy feeling. Go on, sit down for a minute and try it out. Think of something lovely, like your pet doing their favourite trick, or your children opening their first present on Christmas morning, or lying on a beach in your favourite holiday destination soaking up the rays and drinking a glass of freshly squeezed juice, and see how bad it feels. It's simply not possible. I won't ask you to do the opposite, but you get the point. Our feelings come from our thoughts. Simple. What's interesting about this is that we have just assigned the feeling to this thought, in the same way that we assigned the feeling of fear to walking a plank 60ft in the air. It's the same process, it's still being created from the inside-out, only this time we know that we're doing it.

Michael Neill tells a wonderful story about his thinking creating his feelings. He was overseas on a business trip and woke up feeling like he had slept like a baby. That wonderful feeling of rising naturally from a deep sleep is second to none, isn't it? He turned and looked at the alarm clock in his blacked out room and saw that it said: 3am. Immediately, he felt nauseous. A wave of tiredness swept over him again and his mood sank. He rubbed his eyes and looked back at the clock one more time, only to see that it did in fact say: 8am. His mood immediately shot straight back up and the tiredness left him in a flash. If that's not a great example of our thinking creating our feeling, I don't know what is!

One of the ways that we demonstrate this in person is by telling people at our seminars that unbeknownst to them, we have stuck post-it notes under five chairs, and that the people sitting on those chairs will all shortly be coming onto stage to talk. There is an immediate physical reaction from everyone in the room, and depending on the size of the seminar (and the stage), this can vary from slight unease to absolute terror. The ONLY reason for this happening is their thinking. Every one of those people in that room are generating these thoughts, which is brought to life by their consciousness... and they have a feeling as a result of those thoughts. Mind, Thought and Consciousness: the Three Principles in action. If they knew this was happening (through an understanding of the Principles) they would be able to understand their own reactions more fully. They would also understand that they have the freewill to *not* invest energy in something that they have created themselves. They are not at the mercy of the process anymore. They understand that their feelings are only the guide. They are no longer *feeling their circumstances* – aware now that they are simply *feeling their own thinking*.

If you think about a stressful situation that you have had in your life and really go through it in fine detail in your mind, you can actually *feel* something. It's a physical reaction. You are the one creating it though, no one else. It's not the situation that's giving you those feelings, because the situation has already happened. It is only being kept alive by your thinking, nothing else.

Most executives don't know that the 'burden of pressure' is actually informing everything they do. It feels normal to them and part of how they operate. But they are generating it all within their own mind – it's self-created, not job created. They don't HAVE to feel pressure or burden. Stress is *optional!*

Simply seeing the link between this process and the feeling is enough to point them in the right direction. This understanding creates a feeling of humility and resiliency, simply from *knowing* the truth. The feelings begin to dissipate of their own accord and a sense of ease returns, and that's when the wise thinking (or inner wisdom) starts to emerge.

Sandy Krot, a wonderfully gifted teacher of the Principles in the US, tells a great story of a defence company that she worked for in the States, where they had facilitated a training for all of the sales staff. The company had a contract with the US Air Force and had to fly over their sales team to tell the base officers about a delay to a major project. They sat down in front of them and began to explain the scenario. The officers flipped and reacted furiously. Throughout the meeting, the sales team did not react but listened calmly and waited for their own inner wisdom to surface and answers to come. The officers' boss, the General, got straight on the phone to the President of the defence company and insisted that he sent over another team straight away. "*They didn't react, my team tells me that they don't even care... I want you to send me your best team,*" he said. "*I can assure you that they are my best team*" the President replied. "*But tell me, wouldn't you prefer them to be more responsive and less reactive?*" The perception of 'what was necessary' was skewed by the General's own ideas of what was necessary *for him, judging by his own responses* – not the situation. Big difference. Of course, through not reacting and instead accessing wisdom, ideas and solutions arose and the project was finished on time after all — by not getting stressed about it!

So in short, when you're feeling stressed, don't flip out, don't blame, don't shut down, don't try and do anything. Just see it for what it is — thought, created by you... and then do nothing!

Sales

"It's the state of mind of the sales person that determines the quality of conversation, receptivity and experience of the client" – Aaron Turner

Isn't it wonderful that we can now see that business people are running around like headless chickens believing that they are *required* to feel stress in their jobs and assuming this is essential. By gaining an understanding of the Principles, they will realise that they can have full engagement and enjoyment in their work even when the going gets tough.

It doesn't take a genius to see then, that if their thinking is what is getting in the way of them being able to perform their jobs at a higher level, then one of the after effects of understanding the Principles will be better results (through more clarity). When they understand how it works, a great deal of time and energy is saved by doing nothing!

I hear the question asked frequently in business: "*What are the 'bottom line' benefits of knowing these Principles and understanding where thought comes from?*" I refer them to companies with sales staff who have learned this understanding, who experience far greater rapport with potential clients — they are granted more than the standard five minute meeting, or are asked back to present to higher level decision makers, or even get referred on to other companies, without asking.

If a busy executive (who is stressed), meets a sales person (who isn't), they are going to feel it. You know the expression 'desperation stinks'? Well, this is kind of the opposite to that. It's like the antidote to desperation! People who feel better, do better.

I've heard of sales men and women who've had appointments where the executive has blocked off only a few minutes for them but by the end of an hour, the rep is having to cut short the meeting to go to another appointment! It's all about 'state of mind' and where that comes from, which is thought and thought comes via the Principles – every time.

When I work with sales teams, I know that one of the best things that they have going for them is their state of mind, not techniques. If it was all about techniques, there would be 100% effective training manuals handed out to every sales team on the planet! When I ask the sales teams at the intake sessions what is behind their good and bad sales, they think that it's a confidence issue. They look at times when their sales were 'up' and they saw their confidence was up. This reinforces the idea for them that it's the sales that is creating the confidence and lack of sales which creates lack of confidence, and the more they think about this unproductive process, the stronger the feelings get.

For example, if you are about to stand up in front of an audience to deliver an important speech, you might well be one of the 66% of people on this planet who would rather die. The more you think about how nervous you are, the more nervous you get. The feelings you are getting are coming from your own thinking, nowhere else. Yet as you now know, the best way to deal with this is to do nothing with them. See them float on in, remember what they are and who created them and wait for the next thought to come along, just like the clouds in the sky... guaranteed. So just let it. Don't invest any time or energy in the thoughts of nervousness, just 'let it be', as the Beatles would say. Your thinking will always self-correct to default, which is calm and relaxed and your inner wisdom will surface, giving you what you need.

Frequently in the sales process, the outcomes that we attach to it are ones such as: 'If I don't make my targets I will lose my job', or 'If we don't get the contract, the company will go under'. How would you think this would reflect into one's own quality of mind (and subsequent performance) at any given moment? Well, the pressure you apply to yourself, purely from your own thinking, is totally self-created. You apply it, then it becomes real. As we have seen, when this low quality of mind is transferred to the sales process, it's absolutely noticeable from the client's perspective – desperation stinks! When confidence is attached to an outcome and the source of that confidence seems to be created by the outcome, you're into a downward spiral. It is invariably the quality of mind that is the key determinant in the process. Your quality of mind is coming from your thinking, which is coming from thought. Always, always... always! Your confidence is still there, because confidence is the sign of a mind in neutral, it's the natural default state. Look at any young child to see this in action. They fall over, they get up and they carry on without a second thought. Does their confidence take a hit because they fell over? Not a chance.

So what do adults 'do' about confidence? How do we try to get it back to default? Most of us attempt to adjust the *process*: learn a new sales technique or change our state (via alcohol or drugs or watching TV etc), or we vent our frustration at someone else and pass on responsibility. But when you decide you've had enough of this, you 'give in' and eventually get your 'quality of mind power' back, because quality of mind is directly addressable by you, by doing nothing! It's only our *belief* (which is merely thought) that we are dealing with something useful that means we hold onto it (also a thought) in the first place. Without these extraneous thoughts coming into your head and muddying the issue, you would have confidence and clarity of mind all the time. As soon as you realise this at a deeper level, then you understand that most thoughts in your head (when you're not feeling good) are simply not helping you.

When I look at sales teams, I start to see a pattern. The team members with a low quality of mind have lower figures and the ones with high quality of mind have higher figures. It's a pretty clear indicator and it's very accurate. So I ask the sales person or the sales team with the low figures to tell me about a time when they did a great sale, when they had the Midas touch and clients loved what they did. It always emerges that their quality of mind was high, but, they attribute this to the fact that they were doing well. When things took a turn for the worse, their quality of mind dropped and the figures started to tumble. They thought it was the circumstance creating the effect and did not see it as their own thinking.

This is because our minds trick us into thinking that the feelings we are getting are a result of our circumstances, not the cause of our perception of those circumstances. If you fall for this assumption, you can't change your quality of mind or your feelings, unless you change your circumstances, and this is the 'trap' or the 'illusion' that we fall into. So we chase the next thing to make us happy: a faster car, larger house, more money, better job, a new partner, more children, brighter bling, or whatever it is that *seems* to be doing the (temporary) trick. Or, in the sales scenario, we look for a factor outside of ourselves to solve the problem: a different process, or a new product. As we know though, that's looking in the wrong direction, because the relationship between how you feel and your circumstances is purely coincidental.

So I have to show the sales person that their *own thinking* is the <u>key determinant</u> in this process and I do this by showing them the Principles and where their thinking originates from. You see, understanding quality of mind and where it comes from saves you from the limitations of your own thinking. If you don't 'know' what's possible, you can't take full advantage of it for yourself. Whatever you think is possible is what appears to be possible because your thinking is creating your experience. Basically, everything you do is limited by your quality of mind and your perception of reality from one moment to the next, which in turn is limited by your understanding of how the mind creates thought in the first place. Remember the beach in Brazil? Without the understanding of how the tides worked, there would be trouble ahead. And you can't help someone when you lose your own clarity. You're going to struggle to have rapport and build a meaningful relationships if you have low quality of mind yourself and you're not aware of the process behind it.

I lead sales teams to understand that the main factor affecting the relationship that they are having with their clients is quality of mind; quality of mind originates from thought; thought is created via the Principles; and merely having an *understanding* of this is sufficient. So in short, if you are in sales, the best place to start from in the process of getting clients and keeping them happy is one of understanding how the system works. Realise that high quality of mind and low quality of mind are all products of the same process: thought! Moreover, this process has a natural default setting if left alone, there's nothing to change and nothing to do to get back to it.

Communication

I'm sure you've been there – the meeting where it all 'kicks off', tempers are frayed and boil over. Sometimes discussions just don't go well. They get adversarial. When people don't listen well, they don't respond well. Why is that? Is it the pressure of the circumstances or could it be more to do with the attitude of the participants? Might I suggest that the feeling of the participants during the discussions holds the key, and where do feelings come from then?

What if you were in a business meeting where everyone simply realised that they had their own personal thinking going on, and it was interfering with what they *could* be hearing from the other participants? What if simply by knowing this, they were able to let their own personal thinking dissipate (by doing nothing!) and take in (or at least give it a chance), what the other person was saying. How much better would that be? Do you think that issues would get resolved more quickly? The truth is, if you have less attachment to the outcome and more involvement in the moment, then there's more chance that you'll be listening to what others are saying, and I mean *really* listening. Which means everyone's a winner!

I've heard stories of CEOs who've been known to blow a gasket at the first sign of trouble. This was their particular strategy of coping with the issue, which in their mind was stress. They believed that getting angry would somehow ignite others into action. Of course, all it did was increase the stress levels in others and delay the problem solving (through their own innocent misinterpretation of the circumstances). Now do you see how the knock-on effect of the illusion can influence business and the bottom line?

Once they have an understanding of the Principles and how their thinking, and not the circumstances is creating reality from moment to moment – stress becomes extraneous and 'optional'. They realise that their quality of mind is the only determining factor left blocking the way of progress. They describe meetings where a big problem was introduced and instead of reacting and making more waves, they listened, quieted down and came up with solutions way faster than before. Others around them described this as some kind of magic, but as we know, it's not magic – it's merely an understanding of how the process works.

I could go into way more detail on this and give you a whole bunch of other stories and examples to illustrate the point, but I hope that by keeping it short and simple the message will come across. Because the message is really *incredibly* simple: there is nothing to do!

Creativity

"All truly great thoughts are conceived by walking" – Friedrich Nietzsche.

He got it... He knew that by taking ourselves away from the problem, we get a different perspective on it and things look different to us. Personal thought is like driving with the handbrake on. It's going to slow you down and sometimes you're not even aware that it's on at all!

With specific regard to business, it's like taking up 'mental bandwidth' that could be used to pipe creative thought through, solving the problems and finding solutions instead. As I mentioned previously, when senior executives were asked where they got their best ideas, the answers were strikingly similar: *"When I'm on holiday"*, *"When I'm in the shower"*, *"Whilst shaving"*, *"When I'm taking a walk"* – it's often when the mind is quietening down. Conversely, when the mind is stirred up with the waves of thought swirling around, creativity is harder to come by. When personal thinking dissipates, wise thinking shows up.

Robin Charbit, who works for Insight Principles in the US, runs a four day problem-solving workshop called *'Reveal'*. He developed the concept purely by accident at one of his four day Principles trainings. During the second day, the attendees, who were all senior in the company, solved a seemingly 'unsolvable' problem. They already had in the room, all of the data regarding the situation – perhaps too much data. Many an external consultant and even a specialist task force had failed to solve the problem and they were stuck in a rut. Basically, they had been *thinking* about it too long and were too close to the problem. As soon as they got quiet-minded, it was like the rain started to fall and the ruts got washed away. Suddenly, they 'saw' something about the problem that they could not see using the thinking that created it. The answer had always been there, but had eluded them. As soon as they got quiet-minded and had a good feeling, high quality thought came to the surface and insights 'popped' to solve the problem. Robin noticed this occurring and started to use it in other areas of the business with great success, evolving into the product. They are so confident with this now, that the *Reveal* programme comes with a value proposition: either you solve the unsolvable problem in four days or you do not pay!

I hope you can see the power of the Principles at play in business here. It's like we've spent so much time chipping away at a wall to break free, but the wall we've been chipping away at is an internal one. The one that leads to freedom is on the opposite side of the room, and as I mentioned earlier, with teaching an understanding of the Principles, we tend to point people in the opposite direction!

Return on Investment

When Robin first came across his own understanding of the Principles, he happened to be looking for a solution to his own seemingly unanswerable problem. Why was it that business people with a huge amount of experience still make really bad decisions? This is when he came across Syd Banks and the results that he was getting and saw a fabulous explanation of what was *really* going on.

He realised that if people spent more time in a better mental state, their psychological well-being would increase and they would make better decisions more of the time. He also noticed that, as a consultant, people take good advice, and then do nothing with it (but not in the same way that I mean). This seemed to be a universal phenomenon. Most people know how to get fit, lose weight; know that drinking too much is bad for them etc and still choose to ignore it.

He could see that problem situations could get resolved when the people involved produced high quality thinking. He realised though, that most people do not see mental well being as the path to success, especially in business. So to get this new way of thinking across, he had to adapt to how the clients were thinking themselves. What was 'top of mind' for them? How are they currently thinking about it? Where is that thinking coming from? Where does new thinking come from? Which is where getting them to see where their 'A-ha' moments originate, fits in nicely. When they start to see that there are other factors at play here behind their thinking, it's a way to introduce the invisible factor of the Principles and start to get them to look in a different direction. They start to see the internal workings of the human operating system, and of course, when you understand it, you can get more out of it (or at least know the pitfalls to avoid!). The net result of this is specific quantifiable results. Robin's team guarantee fifty to one hundred times return on fees and the client is free to pay whatever they want, including nothing!

A company they worked with recently had a product development process that took three weeks. After the team got an understanding of the Principles, the lead time was cut in half. The net result was a $60 million saving. Not bad eh? Want your bottom line ROI? Well, there it is!

Summary

We are all part of a larger system. No one's mind is more special than, or different from, anyone else's (no matter what you think) and this applies to business too. There is a process at work here that is the same for you and me and everyone else on the planet, and businesses likes processes – they can really relate to this.

The results of having an understanding of this operating system, as soon as you insightfully see it, are that all aspects of the business are affected: interpersonal differences and adversarial discussions reduce, communication with customers improve (rapport), employee empowerment and satisfaction goes up, re-use in the system increases, truancy reduces, levels of leadership and creativity increase and low-and-behold, sales go up! The only thing previously getting in the way of all of this was a deterioration in state of mind and not having an understanding of how the system works. Once this is learned, then you understand how it's best to leave it alone rather than go in and force a change (do nothing) which saves a hell of a lot of time, energy and resource. Peace of mind is the portal to making great decisions. When all the extraneous thinking goes away, clarity shines through. It really is that simple. As Albert Einstein famously said: "*If you can't explain it simply, you don't understand it well enough*".

In business, we tend to look at the processes behind the problem and think that it needs an adjustment to make it right. So we put checks and balances in, but the problem gets worse. It's like looking at the cracks on a wall and assuming that it's a wall problem, not a foundation problem. Of course, leaders who are tense and stressed don't see this – they plough through and make mistakes based on what they know at the time.

With an understanding of the Principles, they see that there is unlimited potential to do well – just take a break from the thinking. When people realise this, they self correct. Once your view of what you're dealing with changes, you don't have to do anything with it, because our realities are actually psycho-spiritual illusions. It's our *belief* in them that creates the problem, and wedged between us and our experience of reality is the creative license of thought. As Syd would say: "*Don't look at the results of your thoughts, look at the fact that you think*".

Our realities are created by the Three Principles – always, without exception. They stand on their own in their own regard, because these Principles aren't concepts. They are a way of talking about a reality that every human being on this planet is dealing with all the time. When we insightfully see this for ourselves, the game is up! The trick is explained. The illusion dissipates and we are free to live without the burden of self-created stress and worry upon our shoulders. It's not a case of casting this aside, it's simply a case of seeing that it never existed in the first place. There was never anything to do. We just made it up!

Best of all, in addition to seeing how the system works, there is an unlimited potential for creativity lying in a well of wisdom available to us at any given moment, which we miss by taking our current feelings and thoughts too seriously, but we can access – simply by doing nothing!

I want to re emphasise here, we are looking at a process that is the same for every human being on the planet. We make up our reality the same way as everyone else. We are alive, we are conscious and we think – *boom* – reality!

For too long, we've been looking at the behaviour of humans. These Principles focus on the 'human' rather than the 'behaviour'. They are 'before the form', the form being: thought, feeling and action. We are talking about a human operating system here. It is profound, huge, enlightening and downright useful! Do you think that if people understood that their feelings were not coming from their circumstances there would be so much conflict? Which brings me on nicely to the subject matter for the next chapter: Parenting!

Chapter Five

Parenting

"Curiosity is a delicate little plant which, aside from stimulation, stands mainly in need of freedom" – Albert Einstein

As is the case with most of the ideas in this book, none of what I am about to tell you is anything new, per se. All I am essentially doing is putting it all into one key message that is easily accessible: do nothing! The same applies to parenting, although this might seem a little strange at first.

A number of the ideas in this chapter are taken from Jack Pransky's *'Parenting from the Heart'* and Ami Chen Mills Naim's *'The Spark Inside'*. Some of those ideas in turn are based on the insights and stories from the other experts mentioned at the front of this book, so the acknowledgement extends to them also. These are both excellent books for parents and I highly recommend that you buy a copy of each. However all of the practical explanations and stories I share involve either me and my children or a close friend or relative and their own kids. In short, this works and it works amazingly well. Let's jump in and get 'down with the kids'!

So when do you think bad behaviour starts? On the changing mat? In the playground? At mealtimes? Let's start with a premise that most of us can agree on. No child is born bad. No child comes out of the womb with 'bad attitude' as standard. At least I've certainly never met, nor heard of one.

What is it then (and I'll use this term purely for illustration) *makes* a child unhappy? Well, you have to look at the first few experiences that they have with their carers to find the answer to that one. Yup that's right, blame the parents!

Babies are born in a naturally happy and inquisitive state. They are born without insecurity, which is something that they learn from their experiences (and from us). None of us do this intentionally, it's just the way it happens. As Jack Pransky explains in *Parenting from the Heart*: as soon as a baby comes out of the womb, it is absorbing a huge amount of information from the word go. There is a whole new world to discover; to see, taste, smell, touch and hear. As soon as they start to feel uncomfortable, such as when they're hungry or have a wet nappy (that's a diaper for you readers across the pond), they tell us. And if yours are anything like mine, boy do they tell us!

Their first lesson, if you will, is that when they cry, a nice grown up will (hopefully) come and tend to their little problem. They figure out pretty quickly that crying is the route to getting their needs met. It's unlikely that any baby, unless in an abusive or neglectful home, will not have this process pretty much ingrained in them in the first few weeks and months of their lives. The insecurity stage starts a little bit later on.

For example, children play with their food – especially young babies. It's just another toy to them – one to be worn or thrown as well as eaten. As soon as the adult (who in this example has not slept properly for weeks) sees this as an annoyance rather than fun (which is just their thinking), the baby gets a telling off. This may not be harsh, just a swift *"NO!"* But just slightly louder than before – with an edge to it. So the baby thinks 'that isn't like Mummy/

Daddy, they've not done that before, I'd better watch out here'. Of course, it is also just their thinking creating this feeling, but they have no way of knowing this yet.

As soon as they start to explore new worlds around them, more dangers appear. When they grab items that can hurt them, the parent stops and scolds the child. The safe world that they have known for their whole life up until now, changes. The happy, peaceful, secure, comforting world becomes slightly confusing. What was once very secure, is now slightly insecure.

Then the child learns to walk, and far greater dangers are now closer to hand; like going for the electrical socket for the first time with fingers at the ready, teasing the cat, or going to pick up a nice warm poo from their nappy and sticking their fingers in their mouth. It's all happened to the best of us (as parents or children) at some stage.

Then, as soon as they become fully mobile, they get scolded for walking off or running (especially in car parks). They start to talk and get scolded for speaking at the wrong times or talking too loudly. The insecurities mount as the child explores new worlds and new dangers, and is firmly shown the boundaries.

In all cases, the way that we as adults react to this, is not dependent on the circumstance, but on our own thoughts or moods, and our understanding of what we are 'doing' with them at any moment. The food analogy works perfectly for this one. At what point do we say *"Enough is enough, I no longer wish to step on mushed up peas and banana"*? It will always vary, *depending* on our thoughts and what we know about *how* we are creating it. One moment it can look like 'the innocence of being a child', and the next they could be 'out to get us'!

My point here, is that our children's insecurity comes from the thinking that they have about the way that we set the boundaries for them. Some children might find their own dangers without the adult even noticing and learn their own way, but it still comes from the thought that *they* are creating. For our part in the process, the more that we can understand how *our* thinking is being created and how easy it is to get lost in the illusion that 'outside circumstances are causing our feelings', the more chance we have of teaching what is good or bad for them lovingly and with care. If we can do this, there will be less insecurity (via thought) for our child.

Everyone is born with innate health. We always have access to our wisdom and common sense, and this includes children! It just needs to be nurtured out of them by helping them see beyond their own thinking, and we can do this by seeing through ours first.

[NB: although children are born with wisdom and common sense, they don't necessarily always know how to access it at any given moment. They need to acquire certain skills and learning upon the way.]

It's the way you tell 'em

So how *can* we do this? How can we provide our children with the best possible environment for them to be able to steer clear of unproductive and unruly thinking and subsequent behaviours? What we want to teach them is how to access their own mental health! Well, what I am about to say might shock you, but <u>no</u> set of techniques will help you have a better relationship with your children — it's like shutting the door after the horse has bolted!

What we need to be addressing here is our moment to moment interactions with our children. What they *feel* from us in the present is the most important factor – what they feel (via their thinking) coming out of us towards them from our hearts, is the key (J. Pransky 2012). If we can see that they are making up their own reality via the Principles and are getting fooled by the illusion (just as we do), we are less likely to get caught up in their circumstances with them. If we can bring them back down-to-earth by talking to their health, we will be heading in the right direction. Essentially, we can tell them anything, as long as it is said with love and compassion, because it's the love and the compassion that they really hear. It's not what you say, it's the way that you say it. If you get angry with your children, at that moment, that's what they are feeling, via their thinking. Angry thoughts ultimately create angry feelings. The feeling we have inside is what they are tuning into. Conversely, if we are feeling love and compassion for them, that's also what they tune into.

Funnily enough, I remember my own mother trying to change my behaviour as a child. My father had left when I was ten and I was rebelling at home and school. We had many stand-offs and a few fist shaped holes in doors in our frequent run-ins.

Then one day, she stopped trying. She just said she would love me and be there for me, no matter what I did and how I felt and despite my lack of wanting to communicate any of my own pain to her. I recall feeling deeply touched by this and our relationship improved. I really respected her for saying it, not straight away but when I had time to reflect and my own wisdom came to the surface. It also gave me the courage to open my own heart more and our relationship blossomed thereafter.

My mother stopped trying to be right or to make me right and decided to show me love and compassion instead. What goes around comes around, because when my own daughter at age five had a really quite terrible tantrum once, I remembered what my mother had said years earlier and decided to show love and compassion instead of disappointment and anger. It worked! She calmed down almost immediately, because *everyone* responds to love and respect.

From that moment on, and remembering the same thing that my mother had done for me, I have always been aware of my feelings telling me if my thinking is off-base when things get tense with the children. Frequently I would forget and those were the times I would get myself into trouble. And those were often the times which the girls would vividly remember – when we ended up quarrelling and me telling them off. So when I learned about the Principles, it all made sense. Now, because I see the process and what's really going on behind the scenes, I don't even have to remember what to do. I just know how it works and the rest comes effortlessly. By staying present and talking to their health and wisdom, the situation improves.

Another example illustrates this point very well. I had my two girls staying overnight with me midweek during term time, so I was due to take them to school the following morning. They both love routine, so getting ready at my house was not the easiest exercise and my eldest was getting quite flustered and lost in her own thinking. Time was ticking on and I was aware that they both needed to be punctual that morning due to an assembly event that was happening first thing. I also needed to be at a meeting early, so I was feeling (and thinking) pressure too. Just as I thought that the situation was under control (hair done, lunchbox approved, teeth brushed), my eldest noticed an ink spot on her white shirt. *"I can't* go to school in this, Daddy... it's dirty!" The other shirt I had for her was also in the wash. What to do..? I could feel my heart rate soar as I looked at the clock. My temptation was to tell her to *"Live with it and get in the car!"* But I could see the tears welling up in her eyes — it would not go well and I would have to end up forcing her to go.

So I stopped. I let that thought roll on by... and a new one popped into my head. *"OK"* I said, *"This is a really good opportunity for us to think about solving a problem together. Let your mind clear and see what you can think of to solve it. Imagine you are Sherlock Holmes, my Darling. You have a case to solve — the case of the ink stained shirt!"* I could see her relax a little and see the situation with fresh eyes. *"Oh, OK Daddy. Erm, let's see... I KNOW!"* She exclaimed after a little pondering: *"Let's call Mummy on the way to school and ask her to iron another shirt for me and have it ready to pick up. Then she can do my hair properly too!"* Brilliant! (and why didn't I think of that?) So that's what we did. And do you know what? Alannah was talking about her 'sleuthing' all the way to school and the next day too. She made up a whole story and a play based on the 'case of the ink-stained shirt'. Where it had looked like there was potential for conflict, there was in fact potential for opportunity, growth and learning.

Another great example of this is from Rabbi Shaul Rosenblatt, who tells a wonderful story of the time he took his sixteen year old son to the theatre. Whilst driving to the play, his son noticed that the time on the sat-nav was wrong and offered to fix it. It just so happened though, that the moment he chose to do this was the same moment that the sat-nav would be telling them to get off the motorway. After his son had finished tinkering, Shaul realised that he'd missed the turning and was forced to take the next exit, come off and return on the opposite carriageway, which unfortunately had a huge traffic jam. His thinking started to play all sorts of scenarios in his head about being stuck in the traffic for an hour, being late for the play and so on. In his frustration, he chastised his son for his (unintentional) mistake. Almost as soon as he did this, he realised that it wasn't his son's fault at all. He was innocently just trying to help. He also realised that they would be sitting in traffic for an hour – no matter what he said or did and who he decided to blame for his frustration. So he immediately apologised and suggested that they spend the time together in the traffic jam playing games and singing – which they did! To this day, both he and his son describe that hour together in the car, in traffic on the way to the theatre, as one of the best hours they had ever spent together, singing, playing and bonding.

So when you get angry or frustrated, just realise where that's coming from. You're the one making it up, getting fooled from the outside-in again, and your kids will end up getting fooled too – because they do what you do!

What you see is what you get

Jack Pransky, in his book *'Parenting from the heart'* says: *"The way we see our children will determine how successful we will be in raising them"*. Or to put it another way: *"What we see is what we get"*. Let's explore this one a little further.

My mother stopped looking at me as a problem child who needed fixing all those years ago and treated me as a lovable person instead – she was looking at me as a healthy individual who was lost, rather than one who required fixing. In turn, I responded in a more lovable way towards her. That's how it works. It brought out of me what was already there.

But what about problem children? What about the ones with serious difficulties, like ADHD*? Even the most troubled children have moments when they act with more health and wisdom than at other times. This means they have the capability within them, so if we treat them from moment to moment as if this is the case, then they will respond better towards us. Everyone, no matter how bad their actions, has some goodness inside of them. I always tell my children, *"It's the behaviour, not the person"*. And what's that behaviour? The *acting out* of thought, of course. If you can see this, and I mean really see it, then it's easier to spot the innocence in them when they get lost, like we all do from time to time. No one is born with insecure, destructive thoughts. They acquire them (well, make them up – but you get the idea). We just have to help them see this for themselves and get them to find their own common sense and wisdom again.

If we look at our children at all times, the way we do when they do something wonderful or funny or cute, or the way we felt about them when they were first born, it will create the environment for a wonderful relationship. If we get caught up in the emotions of the moment, the feelings of upset and distress, thinking that they are 'defying' us again, we realise where these feelings are coming from and we can let them go – we're getting lost in our thinking about the circumstances again. The good feelings are always there, waiting for us to come back to them when our thinking subsides and we return to our default state of peace and calm.

All you need to remember is that we don't have to *do* anything. We don't have to fix what is already perfect. We already have the

---

ADHD: Attention deficit hyperactivity disorder is a developmental disorder characterised primarily by the coexistence of attentional problems and hyperactivity.

feelings of love in our hearts, we just need to let the extraneous thinking subside and there they will be.

I think, therefore I am

Dr Bill Pettit, who does incredible work with all sorts of troubled souls, from rape victims to Vietnam veterans, says of the perpetrators: *"Every single human being at every moment is doing the best that they know how to do, given their understanding and their state of mind at that time"*. Although he is applying this sentence to (in this example) extreme cases, the exact same applies to our children. Our kids are always doing the best they can at the time, given their own understanding and thinking.

So when our children misbehave, it serves their purpose – at that time. Whether it's to push the boundaries or act out of fear or insecurity, it is *their own thinking* that is leading to the behaviour. If they could let these unproductive thoughts out of the way, their natural inner state of well being and calm would prevail.

The late Roger Mills, who pioneered Three Principles work in the US in projects such as Modello and Homestead Gardens, used to liken this return to a natural state of calm, as holding a cork or a beachball under water. Our hands holding it down are the only thing keeping it from rising to the surface. The same is true of our innate health and wisdom – we don't have to do anything 'but' get out of our own way to let it rise to the surface again.

I remember when I was a child and I had borrowed a toy gun from a neighbour's son. My dad told me to take it back but instead, halfway to the neighbours house, I hid it. Later on, when the neighbour and his son came to ask why I hadn't returned it, I insisted that I had brought it back, but eventually was forced to own up and admit that I had hidden it. My dad thought that I had done this so that I could keep the toy. However in truth, I had hidden it because the family in question had two Alsatian dogs that I was petrified of, and I had been forced to take the toy back on my own. My own thinking at that time made sense to me, if not to anyone else. The net result for me was 'a good hiding', as my dad used to put it (and it didn't involve me getting placed somewhere out of the way!) I remember resenting my dad for years because of that.

For children, given what they see and feel at a particular moment, this is exactly how it appears to them and how they will behave. They are innocent to the fact that their thinking is the key determinant factor at play here. If we can help them tap into their own inner wisdom, whilst at the same time help them understand that their thinking is the only thing getting in the way of this, we will be well on the road to parenting success.

We've already seen where these beliefs (which is still just thought) and this thinking comes from. It comes from our children's thinking about us as parents and about the world around them. Children act 'as if' certain things in life are more important than others (G. Pransky) and they get these ideas or thoughts via us. My own mother would (and still does) talk about life 'as if' money is one of the most important factors. In turn, I used to see most things in life in terms of money. It's no surprise that she ended up being a quantity surveyor and value management expert! I always used to think of life in terms of value compared to something else. Looking at clothes, I would compare the cost to either keeping my old rags or waiting to get something as a gift for a birthday, or at Christmas. As a result I would usually look like someone had dragged me through a hedge backwards. I was not aware this thinking was as a result of values (still thought) handed down to me from my mother's 'as if' world. I was entirely innocent in the process. It's no surprise that my brother also used to (and still does) struggle with money.

My ex-wife used to think about family that way – family was the most important thing to her. 'Family always comes first' was her motto. Whatever the belief passed on via thought, there are glimpses of it in use, which we can detect if we look closely enough. Trust, time, security, hard work, survival, the list is endless. As long as we can see this in our children and help them to realise their own innocence (as well as ours), and that they are only acting out of their own thinking – whatever it is and wherever it derived from – we can help them to bypass it and access their own wisdom and guidance.

Actions speak volumes

"OK, I get you, but how can this be applied to children when all hell is breaking loose?" I hear you ask. Don't forget, our kids live in separate worlds from us. They feel differently and think differently to us. They believe at the time, that what they are doing is serving their own purpose well for them. Merely seeing this innocence will be enough for you to feel the compassion you need to help them through it. Please don't take your own thinking too seriously. Don't forget, these programmed patterns (yup, still thought) that we all have, are bubbling under the surface. Most importantly, we need to understand that if we react to our children negatively, this too will be a pattern that they adopt (*J. Pransky*), because the negative thoughts are the only thing preventing the beachball

rising to the surface.

A great way to help you see this is by thinking about what would happen if you were yelling at your child about something – and they fainted. I'm guessing that the issue would suddenly take on a different meaning for you. This happened to me once. I was telling off my eldest daughter for not clearing up her room (as I had asked her to) and my youngest walked in and vomited. Needless to say, the focus of my attention was immediately switched. In fact, I can't remember ever finishing off that particular chastisement with Alannah! We only have thoughts of annoyance or anger when we're not thinking about something else. Simply by seeing, that another thought will be along soon enough, means we can take our current feelings less seriously. In other words... do nothing!

Now, I'm not saying simply ignore the problem or issue, but I am saying that if you do choose to address the issue with feelings of tension and resentment, it will probably make the situation worse, not better. *Remember that love and compassion are where the real action is!*

Mind how you go

I remember coming home after a particularly testing day at work once and tripping over my eldest daughter's shoes in the hallway. I had told her many times about leaving them there and the dangers this hazard could bring to others. But in my mind, on that day – she had forgotten on purpose. Yup, she did it just to get at me! I made a beeline for her room to give her 'what-for'. She was in a great mood, but I didn't even let her get the words out of her mouth. My state of mind was way down low and my thoughts were running riot, so I gave it to her all guns blazing. Did I feel better afterwards? Well actually, no, I didn't. Especially when I found out that she had been in such a rush getting home to race upstairs and make me a drawing to go with the prize that she had won at school; her first ever prize, and one that she wanted to show *me* especially. How bad did I feel? You can imagine – rotten!

Not only then did I have a really bad day, but I dragged my daughter down into it with me, and she had been having such a great day. Lesson learned, big time! This happened before I knew what the Principles were and where all of my thinking is created, but you can see how easy it is to trust your own state of mind at the time, and the consequences this can bring (remember the email analogy?) We know that children respond better when we deal with them from a higher state of mind, one that is responsive, caring and compassionate. What if I had come home, tripped over the shoes, realised that my state of mind was low from having such a bad day at work and that my thinking was off-base, but proceeded to do nothing, go and sit down for a few minutes and let my mind relax and return to its natural calm state? Chances are that I would have been feeling a bit less tense. I might even have forgotten about the shoes and just been wanting to see my daughter's happy smiling face (as per usual). So when I did go to speak with her, I would have been more willing to hear her side of the story before I steamed in (even if I had remembered why I was upset by this point).

What would have happened differently? I would have heard how excited she was and that the 'forgetting to put her shoes away' was an entirely reasonable oversight, given the circumstances. In fact, her state of mind would have drawn mine back upwards even further and I would have been able to see the whole situation more clearly. But no, I chose to take my feelings more seriously and acted upon them first. I would still have pointed out to her that she needed to be more thoughtful in future, but this would have been delivered from a better place, with caring and compassion and loving words and tones. Chances are, it would have been heeded more! The state of mind that we are in, and the tones we use when we deal with our children, are the key factors in determining the effectiveness of our interaction with them. Do you see a pattern emerging here?

OK, so how can we accurately judge if we are in the right frame of mind? Well, it goes back to the feeling – trust the feeling. If we feel light and compassionate – we're good to go. If we feel tight and edgy – do nothing! We might even make the situation worse.

There aren't going to be many situations that need dealing with on the spot, but of course if there is <u>any</u> danger involved it doesn't matter how you're feeling, make it safe! If your child is running out into the middle of the road, don't stop to think about what mood you're in first!

If we can take responsibility for our own thinking and know that the actions we take can have a consequence on our children's thinking, state of mind and their own subsequent actions, we can be great parents to our children.

Listen, we have a problem

Why are some children more badly behaved than others? Bad behaviour is nothing more than insecurity being acted out. What is insecurity? Thought! Low mood and lack of understanding of how it works all contribute to insecurity and bad behaviour. Realising all of this and that the child may not even know what they are doing, all helps us to deal with it more effectively.

Don't forget, children don't want to be in conflict any more than we do. If we can see the situation for what it really is. If we can detach ourselves from it, the chances are that we will be able to *see* the insecurity being acted out, and letting this go will give us access to our own wisdom in the meantime.

If we can listen deeply to our children and not get caught up in defending our own position (remember this from the Relationships chapter?), we might actually be able to hear the real reasons for the conflict and we will know how to respond to them better at that moment (my dad could have done with this advice!) After all, how would we know what is the best thing to do, if we did not understand the situation fully? Look again at the example I outlined about the shoes. I did not fully understand the situation, to my own detriment, which brought my daughter's mood down as well. *If we yell, they react. If we listen, they become attentive.* It's that simple.

So, what are we listening for? Well, if we can hear the <u>meaning</u> behind their words, we're off to a good start. Listen for how they are making sense of their own world or any underlying issues that they might be having.

I found this particularly useful when my ex and I split up. There were a few instances when both my daughters would be playing up. By not reacting and instead listening deeply, I found out that the underlying cause was often insecurity – not knowing what was happening and what the future would hold. This meant that I was able to go to the source of the problem (thinking), not the symptoms (the behaviour). I clarified a few things and made it clear that they would always be OK. It wasn't the behaviour that was the problem, it was the insecurity – via thought. It's not a hard thing to be able to do. Although children use their own language sometimes and find it hard to put things into words, we all have the ability to listen deeply. When your child was a baby, how did you know when he or she was hungry or needed changing? I guarantee that if you ask mothers if they know the difference between two types of baby's cries, most would say that they could tell you immediately.

And what is the best way to deeply listen? Do nothing! Yup, that's right – empty your mind, clear your head and listen, instead of filtering it through your thinking. This can be hard, especially as we tend to (as parents) think of things through 'right and wrong' filters when we listen to our children. If we can just dismiss those thoughts that are irrelevant to our understanding, then that is a good starting place. If we can listen too from a point of view of respect, the chances are that we will hear more than just the words. For example, my youngest told me once that she hated going to school. I had always had the impression that she loved it, but instead of telling her this, I enquired further. *"What is it about school that is bothering you right now?"* I asked. She told me that the reason she hated it, was that her favourite teacher was off sick. When I explored even further, I discovered that her favourite teacher happened to be the one who got the children drawing most of the time and the replacement teacher liked to get them to read more. Further exploration revealed that she was not as confident with her reading and therefore was feeling insecure about school. Hey presto! All that through listening and asking myself productive questions like 'What is she seeing that I'm not seeing here'? She came up with these answers herself. All I did was help her to see them. Two evenings of working on her reading in a fun and friendly environment gave her the confidence she needed to not 'hate school' anymore. Simple.

There's a really fun listening exercise that you can do with your kids. Get them to tell you about school for five minutes (time it) and listen to them deeply. Whenever a thought pops into your head, raise your right arm. Let the thought go and continue to listen and every time another thought pops in, raise your arm again. You'll be surprised how often this happens and the kids always end up in hysterics with all the arm waving. Go on, try it – it's fun!

Teach them what you know

As we have already stated, children react to the quality of our words and our feelings via their own thinking. I remember my dad trying to teach me mathematics for my eleven plus exam when I was a boy. Here was a man who used to get 100% passes in maths tests at school. *"This is the only subject where you can definitely get everything right"*, he used to tell me. So he understood maths very well indeed, but I didn't! Over the course of the weeks and months that he tried to teach me, he got increasingly frustrated at my lack of understanding. However, instead of trying to change the way that he taught me (which was from his own understanding), he merely turned up the volume and kept repeating the same lessons over and over again. The result, as you can imagine, was that I still didn't 'get it' and he became more and more upset and eventually angry at me!

It took a long time for me to recover from those lessons from my father. I spent most of my early school years in the lower classes in maths because I thought I didn't understand it, which ironically hurt him more than it did me. I was his son and he was a superb mathematician. And all because he chose to trust his own feelings and thoughts and not listen to mine. So no matter what you are teaching your children, be aware that the *way you teach* is fundamental to the learning.

That's a fairly basic example, what about teaching your kids lessons about life? Well, the same applies. You should create the right environment for learning – one in which there is an understanding of the process of thought and where our realities are being created. Try to help them to understand the process and then the instruction, in a calm and loving way. Prepare to listen as much as you instruct. Think about how you can show them what you need to teach them and (this is important) make sure that you are displaying the behaviour yourself.

Let's take 'responsibility' as an example of this last point. My eldest was never the tidiest in the house as you might have already gathered. Clothes used to end up all over the place and usually wherever they were taken off! So how did we (ex-wife and I) manage to teach her to take responsibility? At first, Alannah was unaware of the results of her actions. As far as she was concerned, clothes were just clothes wherever they lived! What didn't help here, is that my ex-wife and I also had a bit of a problem with putting clothes away. As far as Alannah was concerned, this behaviour was normal and acceptable. When it got too much for us to bear, the first thing we had to address was our own thinking and behaviour. By making a point of clearing up and tidying clothes, the message slowly started to filter through. You first have to *be for yourself* the results you want to see in your children. Alannah was then able to see that this was more important for us than it had been before.

If you watch any reality TV show involving parents and children, it's usually the behaviour of the parents that needs addressing first. We asked ourselves why tidiness was important to us and explained this clearly to the girls. Clothes need to be treated with respect or they won't last. It's important that clothes are not left out because we all feel better in a clean and tidy environment. They don't tidy their own clothes up at the moment, we do it – but shared responsibility takes less time and is more enjoyable and it's easier and quicker to find things when we know where they are! I'm sure there are plenty of other reasons we could have used (and you could use), but these were the big ones for us. We made sure that we told them all of this when we were all attentive and willing to learn, and nothing that we said was delivered in a judgemental way – it was all done with compassion and love. It was important for us that we did not make this task out to be a chore for them either. In fact, by making a point of the benefits of the process and the fun we had doing it, a whole new opportunity arose for us. All of the old clothes became play items for the girls and all of these were used for fashion shows! The organisation of the clothes meant that they were all more accessible, but we also let the girls help out with the sorting. It was either, colours, styles or eras. The fun that we had in doing this spread to the girls. Before long they had their own systems set up in their rooms and were adhering to it on a daily basis. Occasionally, they would change their own filing system and again make a fashion show out of it. We had green shows, yellow shows, 60's, 80's, you name it, we had it. The main thing is, from that point onwards, clothes were treated with a new found respect because the <u>thinking</u> about clothes had changed.

Discipline? It's all about learning

Another part of teaching them about life is that sometimes they need to get over problems and set-backs. If you've ever been in a supermarket where the sweets (candy) section is situated right by the checkout, you'll understand what I mean. Most kids, already tired from traipsing around the shop, will say that they want a tasty reward at this point. And of course the parent, exhausted from traipsing around the shop, will either give in or stand firm.

If we show them compassion and understanding about their frustration (thought), they will be better positioned to be able to deal with it and move on, rather than being ignored or having what they want. Again, the tone that you use is the most important thing here. Learning to deal with these set-backs is all part of the self-reliance that help children later on in life. The way we teach them, will be the way that they see it for themselves too. We could do the same thing by simply bullying them into submission, like I could have done on that school morning with the ink stain, but this is how they will learn to deal with situations (and other people) themselves when they are the decision makers. The example you set is the one that will be followed by them, don't forget.

Another really good example of this, and one that I'm sure every reader will have experienced, is when you are talking on the telephone (usually to someone important like your boss) and one of your children happens to be in a whiney or raucous mood or just wants some attention from you. If we're too quick to tell them off, to threaten them with consequences or to punish them, we've missed an opportunity to teach the child self-reliance. Explain to them in a loving way that it's important that we are able to hear the other person at the end of the line and maybe even get the person to say something to them to demonstrate this. Explain that giving someone your undivided attention is important. I know this works, because it happened to me with my youngest, Aoife.

Now children below a certain age are harder to reason with than others. Aoife was only three at the time but she got the message OK. She still wanted to be near me and to be involved but she didn't whinge and actually kept pretty quiet throughout. The great thing was, this set up a pattern for the future. She knew that there was more to be learned simply by the tone that I used. By calming her down and explaining gently, she too was able to access her own wisdom from a secure, calm state.

The purpose of discipline is to 'learn', not to punish (J. Pransky). The clue is in the name: *discipline*, which is taken directly from the Latin *disciplina* meaning 'instruction given, teaching, learning, knowledge'. When we see our children getting upset and acting out, it would be best to find out the real reason behind it? If we investigate from a position of curiosity, we are far more likely to discover grounds for the thinking behind the upset. There really is nothing more powerful than being firm without the histrionics. Otherwise, children see this in us when we tell them off and they see that it is driving our own actions. This in turn makes it easier for them to blame something outside of themselves for their own upset. However, when calm prevails and compassion is the driver, it is easier for them to look within themselves with *these feelings*.

This is why children tend to react as they do to being told off harshly. They recoil from the negative energy and kick into damage limitation. They see this as an opportunity to escape, so they run away and hide, or storm off in a huff. Some zone-out and some answer back with the same venom repelled. They are avoiding our attack and protecting themselves. Dr Bill Pettit describes it perfectly when he says that children in these situations, have holograms for ears. They look like they're there but they're not real!

So if we are using discipline as a form of teaching for our children, do we want them to act out of fear, or a sense of knowing what is right and being internally motivated? If we can look at any situation as an opportunity for learning, we are on the right path to teach our children to behave well and act from their own common sense. Conversely, if we use force to discipline them, we are starting a losing battle. The problem is that we can only make this work as long as we're around them. As soon as we're not there, they can do what they want! What happens when they get bigger than us, what does discipline through force teach them then? That bullying someone into doing something is the way forward? So what happens when someone smaller than them doesn't do something that they want?

I recently heard a wonderful story from a very good friend of mine, whom I regard to be one of the most effective parents I have ever met. In fact Wayne and his wife, Carine are probably the best example of everything I have mentioned so far with regard to parenting. Their children are quite frankly, *the* most polite, happy and wonderful children that I have ever had the pleasure of meeting. It's not been easy for them all the way, they've had to work hard at it. But boy, has it paid off. Their son Skai is ten years old at the time of writing and as Wayne is of African decent, he wanted him to read the Malcolm X autobiography. Skai protested before he had even opened the book. *"Dad, it's boring, do I have to?"* *"Just read a chapter a day, and we'll discuss it afterwards"* Wayne said. So

Skai started reading but pretty soon was restless. *"What's wrong"* said Wayne. *"It's the words, they're too long and I don't understand them"* said Skai. *"OK, well any words you don't understand, write them down on a separate piece of paper and we'll look them up together".* Still in a huff, but at least ready to give it a go, Skai carried on reading. At the end of the first chapter, he grudgingly explained what he had read. On day two, he started off again less than enthusiastic but halfway through the second chapter, his posture changed. He began to relax more and concentrate on the words. By the end of this chapter he was positively buoyant. His explanation was enthusiastic and passionate. He was hooked! A few days later, and Malcolm X was all that he could talk about.

So when we talk about discipline, we are actually talking about learning. There is no need and no place for frustration or anger and 'making them do what we want them to do'. Those are the learning techniques that we got from *our* parents. It's not effective, so get off the merry-go-round and try another way instead. <u>Talk to their wisdom from your own place of understanding</u>.

Enough is enough

As I have stated earlier on in the chapter, there are times when enough is enough, when taking control is the only option (like when your child runs out into the road). Young children are simply not old enough to understand danger. Sometimes, when issues are vitally important, the parent has to take charge and draw the line. Children are just not going to be able to access their own wisdom at all times.

Again, it comes back to way that we say it to them. Dr Steve Glenn says: *"We can draw the line with firmness (if we say it, we* mean it), *dignity (not doing it in a way that will embarrass them or put them down) and respect (say it with kindness and caring)"*. And if we can include our children in the reasoning behind our decisions, all the better.

When my eldest was seven, she was invited to her first sleep-over at a friend's house. My ex and I had already decided that eight was the age that she could be sleeping at someone else's house. For us, she was not quite mature enough to take on the responsibility yet – a whole night was a long time to be in someone else's space with her own habits and routines. So we put our foot down. But we also explained calmly and clearly what the reasoning was for our decision. Of course there were tears and tantrums, but for us, this was an excellent example of why we had made the correct choice.

When she had just turned eight, she asked us again, and to test out our theory, we declined. This time however, instead of over-reacting, she simply said that, although disappointed, she was OK with it and hoped that we would change our minds soon. After all, she was eight years old now. Well, that was the mature response we had hoped for, so we gave our permission there and then.

Dr Roger Mills used to say that the point of discipline is to help children regain their perspective so that they can engage their own common sense. Jack Pransky uses a great analogy for this:

> *Suppose a sixteen year old wants to borrow the car. The last time he borrowed it, he left it with a thimbleful of gasoline. If I let him borrow the car again now, he will learn nothing. If I prohibit it with no reason, he will learn nothing. So I might say something like: "I'm not willing to let you borrow the car when you leave it*

without gas. When you do that, I might get stuck. That doesn't make sense to me, so I'm sorry but no."

"Gee Dad, I'm sorry, I won't do it again."

"I appreciate that, I really do, but when you started to borrow the car, I told you that you needed to be sure to bring it home with enough gas in the tank, and you said 'OK.'"

"Dad, I forgot. I'm sorry. Look, I really need to get to my friend's house, he's waiting for me."

"I'd love to let you take the car, but I'm not confident enough that you'll do what I ask. Maybe next time."

My job is to let him know that I mean business here. If he wants the car in future, he'll do what I expect. It's not a punishment, and it's not even stated as a consequence. It's just logical. Because if I'm going to give him access to a lethal weapon, I need to have complete confidence that he knows what is right.

The emphasis here is on logic rather than consequence. They need to see the common sense in our (and therefore their own) thinking. There will always be a common sense solution in every situation that arises, and as we saw earlier with the example of the messy clothes, it is better if our kids can have some input into the thinking behind the creating of the rules and regulations. When children participate in creating the household rules, they take personal responsibility for following them. If a rule isn't working, then use the same process to change it, by being inclusive. Again, any violation of the rules has to make sense to the child from their own point of view. They need to see that adhering to the rules is in their own, long-term best interest.

A really good example of this is at bedtime. We all know that time just before sleep (we used to call it the 'witching hour') when little ones start to get a bit cranky. Dr Bill Pettit describes that fifteen minute window as a prepsychotic state! And we all know the consequences of not acting upon that warning signal. On one very memorable occasion, my youngest Aoife got herself into such a state because we missed 'the window', that she started yelling and screaming and generally tearing up the joint. She was so overtired and yet she just didn't want to go to bed. We were firm with her — but that didn't work. So we tried consequences — that didn't work either. What did work eventually was talking gently on her terms and keeping her safe and secure. Because there was probably an underlying sense of insecurity in there somewhere. She wanted to spend more time with us. If I had known that, we would have saved ourselves an hour of trouble! If I had really listened and not reacted, that is. But this was a time before I understood the Principles, the way that thought works... and deep listening of course!

Another friend of mine used the lack of consequences to his own advantage. His eldest son who is twelve, wanted to stay up late playing on his X-Box. Fed up with policing the nightly sneaky games, he told him that he could stay up as late as he wanted, for as long as he wanted. You can imagine the outcome. Within three days his son was exhausted and going to bed at a naturally sensible time again. His own wisdom told him what to do. I wouldn't suggest this would work for everyone, it was certainly a risky gambit, but there is no one strict rule for everyone. What works for you — works for you. Just follow your intuition and try to talk to their innate wisdom and health... but try to be nice in the process.

Stick to your guns!

A very important point to make here is one of 'not backing down'. If you make the rules, stick to them. Otherwise you are showing your children that you are not credible. If you lose credibility, it can escalate to the point where they won't even hear what you are saying. So if you say something – mean it!

Another friend of mine has a lot of problems with her child over food issues. The consequences that she uses are pretty fair and the tone she uses are calm and loving. But she never sticks to them and always, always gives in, which is why her son runs rings around her. She isn't credible. The father is exactly the same, so it's a no-brainer for the child. He knows the rules, and he sure as hell sticks to them!

On that note, it is unwise to tell children something that is unenforceable in the first place, such as *"If you don't do that thing you will never go for a sleep-over again"*. This simply reinforces your lack of credibility and sets you up for a fall. By the time it really matters, such as when your child is hanging out with the wrong crowd who take drugs, credibility needs to be high (excuse the pun). To start off with, just reinforce the point by saying something like *"Remember what I said would happen if you didn't..?"* This gives them the necessary shot across the bows and allows them time to reflect on what they are required to do (or not do) from a point of their own understanding and wisdom.

It's a wrap

I hope that some of the ideas in this chapter have made sense to you. It's probably the most instructive of the chapters in this book, but I'm not really trying to give you any instruction – it all comes back down to your own understanding about thought and where it is being created – from the inside-out. Still, I hope that it resonated with you at some level.

If we can see that our children are doing it (making it up as they go along) in exactly the same way that we are, we're on the right path. We all get caught up in the illusion that it's the outside world that is causing our feelings of frustration, distress, worry etc. But it never is. There's no exception to this either. Yes, life is a contact sport. Things happen, sometimes bad things, but whatever reality that means for us, is always and only ever created inside us, through the Three Principles of Mind, Thought and Consciousness. When we see this is how it works, it allows us to let the feelings pass without trying to *do anything* with them.

Parenting, along with every other aspect of life, is all about love and compassion and giving. When we can allow this to happen naturally in our lives and let it touch the lives of our children, we're all going to be the winners.

Our children are so important to us. So it would be wise to be able to treat them with the benefit of our own wisdom and help them through life by learning from the mistakes that we made... don't you *think?*

Chapter Six

Addiction

"One of the strongest motives that leads men – is escape from everyday life with its painful crudity and hopeless dreariness, from the fetters of one's own ever-shifting desires" – Albert Einstein

By now, you might have been starting to see the power of being able to realise that your own thinking is creating the world in which you live. In all situations, from work, to relationships with your spouse and children. By simply having an understanding that we all get fooled every day by our own thinking, but that we are the ones who are *doing* the creating, we don't have to *do anything!* The more deeply we understand that this is how the system works, the less we need to try and change it. The system is working perfectly. It is only our misunderstanding of how it is working that gets us into trouble.

It still happens to me everyday. Only recently, I found myself getting irritated with my children. They were (according to my thinking at the time) going out of their way to annoy me – deliberately procrastinating and being late for gymnastics, then lunch with relatives, getting on each others nerves and being 'niggley'! Suddenly it struck me (as it always seems to eventually) – it's *just* your thinking!

As soon as I saw it, my outlook changed. The girls weren't procrastinating at all, they were enjoying playing together more than ever. They weren't being niggley, their spirits were higher than normal and so the dips were more pronounced. When they annoyed each other, it just showed up more. *"Fooled again"* I said to myself. All of that self-created stress just vanished immediately and one thought was all it took.

It was during the very same weekend that I started to think about this chapter on addiction, because on one of the evenings whilst I was still being fooled (and feeling quite exhausted), I remember thinking to myself, 'Mmn, could do with a glass of wine right now'.

Now I was what my mother would describe as 'a happy drunk'. I would always get docile rather than aggressive, which is why I never thought that I had any sort of a problem with drinking. Not like my brother, who would turn in to the world's biggest idiot after a couple of pints. Don't worry, anyone that knows him would tell you this and he would readily admit it himself, which is why he's been sober now for the best part of ten years. You see, being the son of an alcoholic carries it's own stigma but I firmly believe that I got more of my mother's genes, because I would rarely go on binges. I would be far more happy just to have two or three glasses of wine every night, and when I say every night, I mean *every* night.

I worked out once that I had managed about thirty days in which I had not drunk anything at all since the age of sixteen. I knew in the back of my mind that there was a problem somewhere but it wasn't really a biggie, so it could wait. Every time there was an article on drinking too much alcohol, my heart would sink and I would read fervently, only to make an excuse to myself for some reason or other, but occasionally I would stop for a night or two.

On more than one occasion, drinking too much affected my career. One night after a particularly boozy session with a friend of mine, I turned up late for work and was sacked. In my mind, it was just the straw that broke the camel's back and not the main issue, but again, I was only hiding from myself.

Then, it all changed. During the journey of my understanding of the Principles, I realised that all of my thinking around alcohol, was just that – thought. I'm not saying that alcohol is not addictive, certainly taken in large quantities (as with any drug) over a period of time, the body builds up a dependence on it and can suffer if it is suddenly withdrawn*. I realised that my main problem was not as much to do with the dependence on the drug itself, as it was with the dependence on the *effect of the drug* and my *thinking* about it.

I was hooked on the *feeling* that I was getting, and this was coming to me – via thought. This was why I was happy to stop at two or three glasses, but never for more than a day at a time. Then it hit me, that night whilst I was thinking about being able to relax with a glass of wine in front of the telly, 'Oh my God, that's just thought... I'm making it up!' I caught myself doing it again! I had been rumbled! As soon as I realised what it was, the next part was so effortless. I just saw that my thinking was creating the feelings of craving, and let them go. That's right, I did nothing! That night, as soon as the thought popped into my head 'Ooh, glass of wine would be nice', I saw it, put no energy into it and let it fall away of it's own accord, just like the waves on the ocean. Because I had spotted the trick, I could see how I was making it up, even the feelings of craving. I was doing all of it. It wasn't the alcohol at all. The power that I had given it, that it could physically draw me to it, like it had a tractor beam, was all being made up by me in my head. Alcohol itself had no hold over me whatsoever. I had given it this power! Just by seeing where the link had been made, who had

---

*This is not to be confused with how we 'think' about a drug and its effects. Read the passage at the end of the book entitled: Ram Daas gives Maharaji the Yogi Medicine, to see what I mean by this.

made it, and how it had been done, was enough for the 'invisible' chain to disappear. It wasn't that I had to break it, it just never existed in the first place.

So what's the result now? For a while, I rarely drank anything but just recently I stopped drinking completely. I woke up one morning and decided that every time I was having a drink I was poisoning myself. So I just stopped, right there and then. For me, I can see that alcohol in certain situations can be a good thing, like when you're proposing a toast at a wedding, but in general I think of it in terms of putting a poison in your own body and putting the brakes on my life. Alcohol is after all, a toxin, which means that every time you ingest it, your body has to do something to get rid of it. When it does so, it's taking up vital energy that it could be using for something else instead. I may have a glass of champagne or wine from time to time but it's my choice now. I am no longer controlled by my own thinking around alcohol. No twelve step program needed, just an understanding of where thought comes from in the first place! The net result is that these days, I sleep more, get more done, feel better and look better. This is just my own little, microscopic example of how an understanding of the Principles can help with addiction. What I am about to share with you next is the macroscopic version.

The Pioneers of the Principles*

The program of addiction services based on the Three Principles, in Santa Clara County in the United States, is recognised within the Department of Alcohol and Drug Services (DADS) as an alternative treatment and training approach.

In 1994, Robert Garner, the Director of Department of Alcohol

---

*I would like to extend a special thanks to Santa Clara County Department of Alcohol and Drug Services for allowing me to use extracts from Kristen Mansheim's paper entitled: The History of 3 Principles Training (Health Realization) at Mariposa Lodge.

and Drug Services for Santa Clara County, heard about the Three Principles and attended the 1994 annual conference at the Claremont Hotel in Oakland, CA. He saw that the Principles could not only be really beneficial for the addicts but also help his staff avoid the frustration and burn-out that many experienced working with this population.

Principles-based counsellors and facilitators saw miracles happening everyday in their classes. However, DADS, knowing that you were only accepted in the field if you published research, undertook the most scientifically rigorous research conducted to-date on the application of the Principles as a substance abuse treatment. It was a quantitative analysis of the impact of a rigorous course on the Principles provided to substance abusing individuals.

The following is an extract of the qualitative part of this research:

Clients on the Three Principles tract were less treatment resistant (seemed to have less denial and hostility), more motivated to change (moved from external or negative motivation for treatment to internal or positive motivation), had less difficulty and disruption during treatment (less acting out behaviours, including fewer positive urine tests), and completed treatment (positive discharges) at a higher rate than other clients.

Instead of seeing addiction as a disease, this new approach saw it as an innocently misaligned desire for good feeling and relied on the resurgence of one's own innate mental health to displace the compulsion for drugs and/or alcohol. Instead of respecting and simultaneously fearing the addiction, the Principles-based approach encouraged participants to better understand their own psychological functioning as a route to self-navigation.

Instead of seeing one's own thinking as damaged and in need of external correction, this approach taught it's clients to distinguish between their own learned and conditioned unhealthy thought processes and a clearer, wiser and deeper intrinsic thought process that could always be trusted. In addition, clients relapse was viewed in a new and different manner.

From this new understanding, relapse was seen as an innocent attempt to feel good when temporarily lost in an unrecognised unhealthy psychological climate. As a result, clients who were taught the Principles did not relapse as severely, or for as long and returned to appropriate levels of care more quickly and without shame... stunting some of the negative impacts of the relapse.

From a practitioner perspective, rather than seeing clients as sick and damaged, clients were being seen as healthy and whole (and just a bit off track) – and, it was working. Clients in the Principles-based programmes became more self-sufficient, had more self-confidence and exhibited higher levels of well being than their traditional recovery counterparts.

The following accounts are true case stories of clients in substance abuse treatment who have learned about the Three Principles:

Trisha's Story

Trisha is a 51 year old bisexual woman, a former drug

addict. Trisha entered Three Principles tract treatment on May 20th, 2001. This treatment admission was her 54th treatment in total, she had been attempting to get sober since age twelve. Many times she entered treatment freshly raped or beaten. This last treatment began when Trisha had almost died, lost in the Santa Cruz Mountains for three days with no food or water, coming down off of a life threatening physical and psychological addiction to alcohol, methadone and klonopin. She has no recollection of how or why she was even there.

Trisha's family was dedicated to Christian and metaphysical values and was, to the outside world, the model of a loving home. Inside the home, Trisha describes a feeling of suffocating oppression; heaviness and harshness escalated into mental, verbal and physical abuse that tortured her and left her constantly running away from home.

At age eleven, Trisha discovered alcohol, and for the first time, fun; from her first drink, she drank alcoholically – every day, and for the effect. Every night when Trisha returned home from a day of fun, her mother would attack her, choking her and screaming at her for coming home drunk once again.

Rather than preventing Trisha from drinking again for fear of the consequences, it fuelled her drinking even further, pushing her into an isolated world of self-hatred and self-loathing. "No one could hate me more than I hated me. I resented being on earth. I hated life on earth and wanted off. I hated my parents for having me, because they didn't want me anyway. I was suicidal."

Trisha's substance abuse progressed as her life continued. She graduated to more and more substances in ever increasing quantities. Her chemical dependency history includes long term relationships with not only alcohol but heroin, crack, cocaine, benzodiazepines and opiate pain medications.

Staying loaded was her most important goal in life, and as a means to this objective, Trisha found ways to obtain what she needed, whether it be cleaning houses and motels, stealing or prostituting. Trisha, like many others who suffer from substance abuse, also suffered mentally and often, during treatment received diagnoses that included ADHD, severe depression, dementia and numerous personality disorders.

In her drinking and using career Trisha, always violent, enraged and full of hate, often came face to face with the criminal justice system and thinks she was probably arrested between twenty and twenty five times for charges ranging from under the influence to drunk driving, to assault and battery on police officers.

Trisha tried to kill herself seriously fifteen times, with many more near death experiences due to overdosing during blackouts. She injected herself with ammonia and with bleach on two occasions, purposefully overdosed on her antidepressants and tried to shoot herself with a gun on another occasion, leaving a bullet hole in her parent's bedroom wall. She recalls waking up many times in county hospitals after overdosing on the streets and being saved by passers-by who called 911.

In the mist of this world of pain and self-destruction Trisha, at age 37, had a baby. Trisha loved her child and wanted to be a good mother; her child was the only reason she felt she had to stay alive, and yet she knew deeply that she was in no position to care for another human being. Eventually her child was placed with family, and Trisha, knowing this was best for her baby, could only hate herself all the more for her failures and inabilities. Her substance abuse reached new lows during this time, and she lived on the edge of death as a lifestyle.

When she checked into rehab for the final time, barely consciousness, Trisha remembers that she felt people cared 'about her', not the condition she was in, the position she'd put herself in, or the advice she'd ignored. Trisha felt a genuine concern from the staff, and a feeling of hopefulness for her, despite her relapse history.

She could tell she was being seen as healthy, as a person with possibilities, and not being seen for her behaviours, her difficulties or even her personality. "People loved me even though I didn't love myself. I felt so much love I just felt like I couldn't let the staff [who believed in me] down."

In treatment, Trisha's physical and psychological wounds began to heal as she learned the Principles. She learned that each human being, including her, has within them a wellspring of mental health that is accessible at all times; this health cannot be created nor destroyed, it just is. And that her mental health could only be held at a distance from her temporarily through the use of the power of

Thought brought to life by Consciousness.

Coping mechanisms that had saved Trisha, and yet almost killed her at the same time, slipped away. Her mental well being reemerged and she began to make decisions she had never before considered: engaging with her mental health team, taking medication and working in tandem with her doctor to adjust her dosages, accepting disability as a safety net to allow her access to services and support in the community until she was strong enough to return full time to the work force; staying away from unhealthy relationships and forming friendships with sober people, and finally, slowly, contacting her family and her child to earn their trust and faith.

Today Trisha has a life she never imagined that she could have – she sees her child regularly but does not disrupt the stability of his home. She is maintaining a chemical free life and now works full time helping other women just like herself. Her cognitive functioning has repaired itself. She is happy to be alive; she enjoys her life and is glad she is still on the planet. Above all she is grateful that something new emerged within the field of dependency treatment, something new that helped her save her own life.

Arianna's Story

Arianna was born in 1970. Her family life and early years were difficult; there was a great deal of anger, frustration and disconnectedness, as well as frequent physical outbursts. Arianna's late teens and young adulthood years included two involuntary commitments to psychiatric lockdown facilities, at least ten separate stays in juvenile hall, multiple group home placements and in her adulthood, more than twenty arrests for various drug related offences.

Her doctors diagnosed her with post traumatic stress disorder and bipolar disorder. Arianna tried to kill herself numerous times, at one point almost losing her arm from an abscess due to intravenous drug use that spread towards her heart. She contracted hepatitis and in the late stages of her using, became critically ill.

In the county jail, Arianna was mandated to a series of classes that included a class that taught the Principles. She describes the majority of the classes there as painful or not helpful. This class, however, stood out as different to her.

"I looked like I was present and accounted for, but I wasn't. I was in a fog. Being in and out of custody so often, everything was a blur to me. But this teacher's class, it did something to me. Her class was the only class I wanted to go to because I liked the way I felt there. It was different. For the first time, I wasn't treated like a case or a number, or given a label. I was told I had wisdom – It was a completely different message. It was completely opposite from my other classes."

"It was confusing because my other classes told me something different; they told me that I was sick and needed to work on myself. I knew I liked the Principles class and that they were telling me the truth – I could feel it. But because I was attending other classes that told me the opposite of the Principles, the message wasn't pure; it wasn't consistent. I think that's why when I got out, I got caught back up." Arianna was released from custody, and was picked up by her boyfriend who was still using.

She picked up her old life where she left off and got caught up again using, landing in jail once again – this time having stolen a car and been picked up under the influence. "I knew what to look for this time though," she says. So Arianna went straight towards Principles classes, and listened to the instruction about her psychological health. This time, upon her release from custody she was mandated to a drug treatment facility.

At the residential treatment program, during her first ten days in treatment, Arianna was given traditional Twelve Step based treatment. She found herself intensely dissatisfied, feeling once again not helped and seen by professionals as sick. Remembering her experience with Principles classes while in custody, she approached the administrative staff demanding that she be allowed to change therapeutic milieus or else she would leave treatment. As she was mandated by the court, that would have meant Arianna going straight back to jail – but she didn't care.

"I couldn't tolerate the negative approaches to getting better. I knew it wouldn't work for me, and not because I had an attitude, but because I instinctively knew the truth."

After two weeks of twice a day classes in which the Three Principles were repeated to her over and over again without the interference of other approaches, Arianna says, "I woke up one morning and came to class, and as the teacher was talking about the Principles. I was overcome with this beautiful feeling. I became completely clear. Not intellectually, but in my heart. The weight of thirty two years of a traumatised psyche vanished and I was released. I understood that I was healed and the healing came from inside of me, from this beautiful feeling. I went into a state of pure well being. My mind got totally still for a minute and I got well. My mind peeled back and I saw what I had been searching for and that it had been there within me all along."

Until this experience, Arianna reports she always struggled with cravings for drugs, which she never felt she could control. Instead she would simply resort to getting high to relieve the intense feelings of anxiety inside herself. One of the things that surprised her most was that after her insight, the idea of drugs no longer occurred to her. "My cravings disappeared completely. All my compulsiveness left me. I felt sick thinking about drugs, I didn't even want them."

Five weeks into treatment Arianna left the safety of the facility on a pass to appear in court. Whilst outside the court room, Arianna was offered drugs by a friend from her past. She remembers watching her own mind create a craving, which she says lasted inside of her for several hours. It was the first time she had ever experienced craving and not used. She credits her ability to wait out the craving to her understanding of how the human mind functions to create reality.

"I didn't have to use, because I understood where my feeling, my craving, was coming from. I saw the memories come into my mind as thoughts, and as that happened I felt myself get sick in my stomach. Then I had a brand new thought, the thought that I didn't have to use. It was a jump in my understanding. I saw thought in action, like a movie. I saw thought, creating. My physical body was feeling my thought. My physical body had nothing to do with life or the drug, but just my thoughts. It wasn't seeing the drug that triggered me, <u>it was my own mind</u>."

"My main prison in life," she says, "was my mind. No one had ever explained my own mind to me. Never had all the other ideas and concepts and theories been completely set aside for me to just get some time to consider the truth – just the truth of how my own mind had been holding me hostage. I finally knew what real control was, the good kind of control. I felt pure positive power. I saw the danger was not outside me, but that the danger was only my own thoughts."

Not only did Arianna not use, she returned to treatment to share what she had learned, and to continue to learn more. "All it took for me to be healed was to understand. And what it took for me to understand was to be in an environment where someone else who understood, could explain it to me clearly. I was pointed to the Principles behind my life, not to the destruction in my life. There was nothing in my life to help me – looking at that did nothing for me except make me feel bad. I needed to know where it all came from. The mental and emotional distress

I was experiencing didn't come from my family, my life experiences or anywhere else... it came from how my mind held the experience and what it meant to me, and all that was within my own mind."

Today Arianna is an A student in college, has completed several years of training to be an instructor of the Principles, and now teaches people what she knows about them, as well as health and well being. Of her own understanding, she says, "Not only was it life saving, but this understanding has given me the ability to experience a quality of life that is far beyond what I had ever imagined possible for someone like me."

Bernadette's Story

Bernadette's story completes our trio. Her life is an example of the unknown power of the Principles to affect not only psychological well being, but physical well being as well. Whilst being another woman who looked hopeless under the influence, she has shown the power of human resiliency, regardless of circumstance or condition – including relapse.

Bernadette is a 'professional', a career woman who is now in her late 50's. She was raised in an idyllic middle-class home that she describes as 'high in expectation and low in tolerance'. She was raised to be polite, to succeed and achieve, while also marinated in a bigoted and prejudicial ideology.

Her rebelliousness against her family's fixed and rigid ideas, which initially protected her from adopting the family philosophy, evolved into a way of life for her, an obsessive, 'you can't make me' attitude which included a complete disrespect for all authority. She was pregnant with her own child by age seventeen and had already embarked on her career of emotional 'fixing'... a career she nurtured alongside her work career.

She fixed with men, she fixed with working, with being a 'star', with making money, with getting married (four times) and with drinking a lot.

By her late thirties she was ill from her alcoholism – much to her own surprise. A series of blackouts (conscious behaviour that is unrecorded in memory) coupled with the obvious and embarrassing lapses, as well as a severe physical dependence on alcohol, illuminated her unrecognised shift from 'liking' drinking to 'needing' alcohol to physically and psychologically make it through the day.

Bernadette found some sobriety with Alcoholics Anonymous but relapses for her were common. Her longest time sober was six years.

In 1996 Bernadette was given devastating news; her increasing levels of physical pain were explained by rheumatoid arthritis.

For several years after the diagnosis she continued to stay sober, but eventually the tedium of day-after-day pain issues led her back to the desire for numbness promised by alcohol. At age fifty three, sick from alcohol and after seventeen years total of Twelve Step recovery, including diligent step work, faithful meeting attendance, being sponsored and sponsoring others, Bernadette entered a Principles based treatment tract – a last ditch attempt to offer her something new, in the hope that it would help a woman who had already received the best the field had to offer.

Bernadette thrived in the new program, learning things that were eye opening for her. In one of her first Principles-based treatment groups, Bernadette remembers one of her counsellors leaning over to her and telling her, "Bernadette, you aren't broken."

She calls this her 'landmark moment' – the moment when she first saw hope. When asked why that statement was so important to her she replied, "I had been in the hospital ER's for years because of how sick I was. I was dying – dying from my drinking and deteriorating from the arthritis. I had no confidence that I could get well again. I had tried to get sober for eighteen months straight – tried and failed. That was the first time I saw myself differently. I saw hope."

That moment allowed Bernadette to become interested in learning something different. She had not realised there was a new approach to addiction entering the treatment field. She was interested and hopeful enough to listen. She attended regular lectures on the Principles of learning about Mind, Thought and Consciousness. "Next I heard about THOUGHT. Not my thinking, but THOUGHT! I noticed that what they said was true. I was doing the creating. I noticed, just around the facility, how much I was making up and it propelled me into a state of ongoing insight. I recognised the 'habits' of thinking that were part of my addiction, too."

"Now keep in mind, I had been on a spiritual pursuit all my life, attending workshops, classes, churches, following new age philosophies, astrology, meditation, anything I thought would help me. And so the idea of 'Mind' settled in nicely for me. We are all connected to life energy. That's true. When I heard the science of it, the logic spoke to my own personal spirituality."

"Understanding three psychological Principles helped with the intense busyness in my head. I had been so busy for so many years and as I saw this was me, in the moment, making up so much, it got quieter up there. Living in reality is remarkably simple. It's much easier than it was to live in my head."

"I realised the difference between 'coping' and 'recognition' – coping with all the stuff I made up, thinking I had to deal with it all, and realising that I was the thinker. That one truth changed everything. I realised how joyful life can be. I realised that in order to struggle with anything, I first had to make up ideas about how (or who) it 'should be'. Now I know the experience I'm having is being 'created' by me, so I'm not so terrified of it. It takes the fear away; I can see how silly most of my ideas are. That I'm the creator, now there's one Principle for every occasion – it applies to everything!"

Bernadette completed treatment and transitioned to the community with a new found sense of peace. Recovery was now simple and easy for her, and to date she has had six years sober. She feels that the place of recovery she has found now is very different.

"If I'm accelerating in my head, if I'm not peaceful, it gets my attention really quickly. I've had more peace in the past few years knowing how my mind works then I had in my whole life, even in my years sober."

"When I was drinking, I was coping with my biology. When I was sober [before], I was coping with my psychology. Now, I'm not coping with anything; I'm at peace. I'm calm. I'm not thinking about drinking or not drinking – drinking one way or the other isn't in my mind anymore. I respect that my biology cannot tolerate alcohol and that's the end of it. There's nothing else to think about! I don't have to do anything!

Interestingly, especially to her doctors, is Bernadette's progress with her rheumatoid arthritis. This woman, once unable to walk, nearly crippled and heavily medicated, has gone two thirds of a year off all arthritis medications. She attributes this amazing physical progress to a knowing about her herself, "Before I was under the constant illusion that I needed something to be ok... a guy, a job, a book... something. I imagined my well being was somewhere – somewhere else. Now, my well being is never missing. And I also know I am not my body."

Today Bernadette stands strong and stable; she works full time at a major university and calls her job the 'job my whole life has prepared me to do'. In her spare time she teaches classes on the Principles to women addicted to alcohol and other drugs. She has written many short *essays on the Principles and her experience of physical pain, and she is an award winning poet with a published book of poetry to her credit.*

Three incredibly powerful stories to highlight the amazing potential that an understanding of the Principles has, to really change lives for the better, even in seemingly hopeless cases. The Principles approach is a smooth path to understanding the cause of addictive behaviour *via thought,* and getting back on track to enjoying our lives again. It focuses on the health we all have inside us, rather than the addiction itself.

Everybody thinks crazy thoughts from time to time. When we feel trapped, it's as a result of our thinking, not our situation and therefore our discomfort is basically an accrual of a lot of our own thinking. We then do all sorts of 'actions' to negate this feeling, be it drinking, smoking, shopping, gambling, over exercising, over eating, bulimia, affairs, whatever.

If you understand that the sensation of needing to 'do something' to clear your head, is also just your thinking – you are able to see it with clarity and not put any further energy into it. If you're overwhelmed by thought and want it to go away, you sometimes do crazy things to go with the crazy thoughts. But by doing nothing, we can let our minds return to their natural calm state, without intervention.

In my case, by simply 'seeing' that it was my thinking creating the feelings of stress and then creating the craving for the alcohol as the medicine, rather than working unnecessarily hard to overcome the desire to drink, I realised that I had made it up to begin with. It wasn't the stress or the alcohol, it was me all along!

An understanding of the Principles is therefore based on the natural laws that govern our psychological make-up rather than a process that needs to be *applied to us* to work. Once understood, our innate health and well being can be accessed to guide us through life, to make choices and decisions that serve us in living a creative, productive and positive life, instead of a selfish, destructive one.

My own understanding led me to see this choice for myself – the 'inside-out' method. Now I don't have to do anything. I know what's happening, so I let it happen. The Principles offer a solution via understanding and insights rather than steps to follow, or techniques to apply. We are all the world's best expert on ourselves, and there really is no one outside of us that can ultimately guide us back to full health. As one Three Principles former addict states: *"I've done a lot of drugs in my time, but nothing felt as good as my experience of the Principles."*

The three stories you have read within this chapter are immensely powerful. It is my desire that they give hope to those who might be currently suffering from addiction *via their own thoughts.* There is hope beyond your current thinking!

Chapter Seven

The Three Principles (part 2)

"To seek Truth from the form alone is only half the truth. As the human mind ascends in consciousness, the oneness of life emerges. There is one Universal Mind, and wherever you go, it is with you, always" – Syd Banks

Throughout this book, there is reference to an inner source of wisdom that anyone can attain at any given moment. You may at some stage in reading it, have experienced wisdom coming to you via an insight or idea. It may have arrived in small ripples and it may have come in a sudden rush, but I hope you have had the benefit of its presence at some stage.

Now, where do you think 'it' came from then? Somewhere deep inside your soul perhaps? OK, so where did that come from then – your soul I mean? I touched upon this very question in the first chapter about having the ability to understand something new for the first time. This is where I will explore it a bit further.

I'm going to make a bold statement here. The source of wisdom I refer to is connected to the same source that created the whole universe. In the world of physics, energy is subject to the 'law of conservation of energy' which states that energy can neither be created (produced) nor destroyed by itself. It can only be transformed. The total in-flow of energy into a system must equal the total out-flow of energy from the system, plus the change in the energy contained within the system. This law is a fundamental principle of physics. Put differently, yesterday, today, and tomorrow are physically indistinguishable, when it comes to energy, that is. When it comes to the energy that makes up who you are, from your physical body to the life force energy that gives you life, to the soul that gives you spirit, it is all energy that was here yesterday and will be here tomorrow, as an indistinguishable force. You have always been here, and always will be – *in one form or another.* As Einstein said: *"The distinction between past, present and future is only a stubbornly persistent illusion".*

The energy that created the big bang, 13.7 billion years ago, when we were all part of the exact same energy as we are now but in the size of a primeval atom, is the same that is present today in all of its different forms – from far away galaxies, to the ends of the universe, to the discarded chip packet on the road. It's all the same as you and I. Every single bit of it.

We are all part of what people call 'God' or 'Tao' or 'Great Spirit', or however you like to describe it. It doesn't matter what you name it, it's still that elusive 'Truth' I referred to earlier. We are all made of it. In fact, we are it! The single most powerful force in the universe lies within each of us. The same thing that gives life to you is the same thing that gives life to me and is the same thing that is life itself. It is all connected, as we are all connected.

In physics, there is a phenomenon called 'Quantum Collapse' or 'Entanglement' which happens instantly regardless of distance. If two entangled particles are separated by millimetres, kilometres or even the size of the known universe, the communication between the two particles is still instantaneous. Spin one particle, and this will cause the other particle – no matter how far away it is – to instantly acquire the other state.

So we are all connected at a deep level. We are all one, whether you like it or not. *It is only the illusion of separateness that disconnects us.*

Having an idea of this amazing oneness gives us a clue to where all of this wisdom comes from. It, like us, in one form or another, has always been here and always will be. You can trace it back for yourself if you want to understand it logically. The life force that your mother and father gave you through conception was given to them in turn by their own parents. This has been passed down through generations for millions of years, through evolution and changes in species and the very nature of the planet.

Where did it originate? Well, some scientists believe that an asteroid fell to earth which contained water, the life giving element previously missing on the planet, and wherever that asteroid came from was the next link in the chain. But wherever it came from, somewhere back in the distant past of our existence, there was a life force which began 'life' as we know it. Who knows what came prior to that. Perhaps it has always been here and we just can't get our heads around there being an infinite life source.

Whatever you believe to be true for you, one thing you cannot deny is that there is some sort of intelligence at play here. Little babies have an inner guide that lets them know what to do, when to cry and how to start to grow the right bits and bobs. Trees 'know' when to grow fruit and when to shed their leaves. Squirrels know how and when to collect nuts for winter – they don't need to read a manual to get this knowledge.

This intelligence is inherent in everyone and everything already. I have no idea what this universal intelligence is, where it came from or what it plans to do with us, but I know that it's there. And if you think it isn't, just ask yourself, 'What is giving me the power to think that it isn't'? 'What is giving me the power to think at all...'? You see, there's no escaping 'it'. It's either there and you're part of it, or it's not there and <u>you've</u> created it all. One or the other! If we're conscious, by definition, we're creating.

When we start to see that our world and the way we create it is essentially 'the wrong way around', that we see things from the outside-in, instead of the inside-out, then the world starts to look a bit different. At least it did for me, and the countless others I speak to who now have this understanding. We don't see life happening 'to us', we see it happening 'through us'. We <u>are</u> life.

Just think. Now, as you are reading this passage, is the only moment that there is. Everything that has ever happened in the universe for an infinite amount of time prior to this precise moment has led you to this place and this time, doing what you are doing right now, has led to you reading this, right now! How amazing is that? There is nothing <u>but</u> now. This is <u>all</u> that there is.

One lady whom I spoke with at a recent training said to me that she thought that none of what we see as 'life' or 'universe' is at all fascinating. She thought we were all here as a fluke and that it was just 'so' and that was that. There was no mystery to it, nothing special to know or understand. We live, we die, that's it, no more. I asked her if she ever felt in awe whilst looking at the world, or at people, or even at a sunset.

"Not really", was her reply. *"Well, if that's the way you see it, then that's the way you see it"* was my response. I'm sure one day, she will look down into the eyes of a new born baby and see what I am alluding to. But then again, maybe she won't.

Because what you see is what you get. There was nothing I could have said to get her to see it differently, she will have to have that insight for herself. In her own understanding, that was what it meant for her. When I pointed out the physics behind energy and the fact that we were all one once, she just said *"Well, I don't feel it"*. When I explained to her that it is impossible to have an intellectual picture or accurate model of 'Universal Mind', because that model is itself made up by Mind, she didn't see that either.

As Vernon Howard once wrote: *"A small child is more attracted to a shiny stone than to an unpolished diamond because he does not know the diamond's value. So it is with the unawakened man. He scorns or ignores cosmic facts. He does not know that he does not know."*

The thing is, at least it was for me with the Principles, is that you get a glimmer of light, something that doesn't sit well with all of your previous understanding. Something that makes you scratch your chin and say *"Mmn, there's something in that"*. And that's when your journey begins. Once you begin to realise (by means of your own insights) how the Three Principles work to create your own reality from moment to moment, your own reality begins to reshape itself.

If you look at all the 'enlightened beings' that have taught and spoken about life, they have all had similar experiences. Their own 'waking up' occurred by seeing what they already knew, differently. Seeing the 'truth', for want of a better word, about how it's all put together, what it all means and why we are here.

Syd Banks once told one of his students that *"The Truth can never be understood. It can be realised, but never be fully understood or told"*. Because, as soon as you put it into words, it's lost. Words cannot describe the immensity of it all. Where did we come from? Who or what made it? If it is infinite, what does that mean? And wouldn't this just be the tip of the iceberg anyway, even if we did know?

As I always say when I talk about the Principles with anyone, *"There are three facts, and anything I say after that is just my opinion"*. It's up to you how deep you want to go. The 'rabbit hole' is infinitely deep, I believe. Just like the levels of consciousness and awareness, or the amount of thoughts that could be created at any given moment.

As you can probably see by now, looking at the results from the chapter on addiction, there is great freedom in having an understanding of these Principles. It's a realisation, an awakening to something way bigger than all of us. We are already perfect, we just don't 'think' we are...

There is a film called *'The Shift'* which stars Dr Wayne Dyer, who plays himself in a semi-autobiographical role about himself (and life). I highly recommend it. If you have seen it already, watch it again. I saw it for a third time recently and realised how much further I had come on my own journey because I saw so much more in the film this last time, because my own level of consciousness had risen.

Many of the messages in the film are very similar to the Principles and in fact a lot of people say to me *"Well, it just sounds like this or that"*... and it does. What it alludes to is very similar to a lot of teachings you may have already come across: Buddhism, Taoism, Zen etc. They're 'inside-out' too. Ultimately though, the messages are the same. It's all about being connected back to the source, to the creation of it all and realising this as the path to your own enlightenment (and whatever that may entail).

Your own connection with the source is what I allude to here.

When you realise that you are not separate from it, you will begin to understand the true nature of your own existence. At your core, you are the same spiritual essence. <u>The world 'outside' is a reflection of the human mind and is an illusionary gap between the spiritual and the physical</u>. By doing nothing you are allowing the silent working of your mind to bring the inner self and the outer self together. I wish I could say that it is more complex than that, but it isn't. We just think it is!

Be still, and know that your spiritual self, or your soul, is part of the divine intelligence of the universe and as such, has infinite power. The more you trust it, the more you are taken care of. As you ascend in divine consciousness, the gap between the spiritual and the physical narrows and the oneness of life, your own existence and your true spiritual identity will start to emerge.

Chapter Eight

Sport

Morpheus: "Don't think you are, know you are..."

I mentioned stress in an earlier chapter, with a specific reference to taking a winning shot in golf, or basketball or whatever requires a level of performance. This chapter delves deeper into that very subject matter. Because when there's a whole tonne of money, pride or success on the outcome, it matters! At least, that's what one might think...

One of the leading authorities on the Principles in sport is Garret Kramer, the founder of *Inner Sports, LLC*. Garret has been a consultant to hundreds of well known professional athletes and coaches – from Olympians and teams, to high school and collegiate players across a multitude of sports. [For the sake of this chapter, I will refer to all of the above, including amateurs of every ability as: 'athletes'.] A former collegiate ice hockey player himself, Garret has been featured on many leading sports radio shows such as *WFAN* in New York, *ESPN Radio, WOR, FOX, CTV*, and also in the *New York Times, Wall Street Journal* and *Sports Illustrated*.

Some of what I will share with you here is from Garret's book: '*Stillpower: The Inner Source of Athletic Excellence*'*. I highly recommend it, especially if sport is your main 'field' of interest (excuse the pun).

Garret describes the 'state of mind' that we have been referring to in previous chapters as "*Stillpower: the clarity of mind to live*

*Usage of extracts from this book have been kindly permitted by the author.

with freedom and ease; the inner source of athletic excellence". So how do we 'prepare' for this? What do we have to 'do' to get to this place? The place that sports people often refer to as *The Zone*.

Well, I guess you might be able to take a shot at the answer by now. That's right — do nothing! It's not somewhere you have to get to, it's already there inside of you. Let's delve further into this and see what we can uncover.

It is widely recognised that the standard method of approach taken by coaches and trainers across the globe has been to 'rev up' or motivate their players — or conversely get them into a state of calmness before matches. However, revving up a player doesn't always work and neither does calming them down.

Revving up can work sometimes, but other times it can lead to all sorts of wayward decision-making which results in poor performance. Likewise, relaxing a player can sometimes work and sometimes not. It's all a bit 'hit and miss'.

In both cases, the coach is relying on 'outside-in' techniques. They believe that external circumstances are affecting internal behaviours and as you know by now, that isn't the way it works... ever! Including in sport. Because the secret to success does not lie in a method or a technique, or the right kind of pep talk or a lucky charm! If it did, we'd all be using it.

Now, I'm not saying that preparation isn't valuable. Of course it is. Training is necessary. Practice is necessary. Learning about the rules or what to do at certain times is necessary. Preparing the physical body for the task ahead is necessary. I'm talking about the mental side of the game here, the winning mentality.

So, if there is no technique, we're back to having an understanding about the big picture again, which in turn brings us back to the

Principles. When we know where our thinking is coming from and that we have nothing to do to get it back to default, we're on the right path.

When an athlete is performing at his or her best, there is a 'clarity of mind' and ease about it. Yet so-called experts, who believe in the outside-in approach, think that it is the athlete's performance that is the source of their state of mind. How does this work when the athlete has been performing well and then suddenly performs badly? What causes this drop? It can't be his performances, because they were going well. Therefore it can *only* be his or her state of mind (which is thought). Remember the section on sales in the Business chapter?

Garret uses a lovely metaphor to explain this. A poor performance and the feelings associated with it are like driving around in a car with the engine warning light on. The athlete has three options (for the sake of this metaphor anyway). He could simply ignore the light and keep driving, which would no doubt end up in a hefty garage bill. He could realise that the warning light is just that, a warning, and take it to a mechanic to get it fixed. But then something else goes wrong eventually and another problem needs fixing (I had a car just like that once). Or, he could find out the inner workings of the machine itself and 'know' what was wrong with it, so that if anything goes wrong again he can fix it himself.

Again, I want to highlight here that this is just a metaphor. There is nothing to fix and no fixing to consider. It's an understanding of the process that is key here. In the case of 'mental performance', the Principles do just that – they explain the workings of the machine. They let us know that the thoughts that we are creating are all part of the process, *not the end result*. As soon as we misinterpret them as being the end result, we think that we need to change them, when actually there is nothing to change. Just having an understanding of the process lets us see this quicker and prevents us from putting energy into having 'concern' about trying to change things. We're back to trying to *change* our thoughts again. It's simply not necessary, there is nothing to change.

The problem for most people (especially coaches and trainers) is that this seems counter-intuitive. We've been conditioned to 'fix' stuff straight away. If it feels bad – change it. If a player feels nerves before a game, and then has the mistaken belief that the nerves will affect his or her game, they are putting energy into the belief and compounding the problem. Simply recognising that thoughts and feelings create our realities will render the need to alter those feelings powerless. Some athletes take nerves before the game as a good sign – it is preparing their bodies for action. It all depends on what energy we put into those thoughts, and just knowing this makes all the difference.

Let's look at the two sides of the same coin in more detail. When athletes are asked what high performance feels like, they describe it as 'natural', 'freedom', 'coming out of nowhere', 'requiring no thought'. Conversely, when they describe poor performance, words like 'trying', 'cluttered', 'bound up' and 'overthinking' emerge. As we have already mentioned, coaches and trainers believe that to get from one of these feeling states to the other, there is a process involved. But the player's experience always results from his or her own thinking and ensuing feelings in the moment. When performance levels drop, the worst thing that the athlete can do is go searching for a fix. It's an easy mistake to make though, because coaches and players react to failure in the same way as they do to temporary triumphs. They are focussing on the event and becoming passive victims of life itself.

What do they do? They put their hopes in a mental exercise, psychotherapy, visualisation, or even a magic pill. These methods might work once or twice, but then the athlete relies on them to work again. He or she is looking in the wrong place. That's not where the answer lies. Time and again, the explanation comes from the inner self, because when effort is unbounded, athletes don't even think about trying hard. How often do we hear them say afterwards: *"I don't know what happened today, I was just in the zone"*. So what is this 'zone' that they keep referring to? Garret describes it as: *"The place where external limitations cease to exist"*. It's the place where there is freedom, where athletes don't think, they know. They don't focus, they feel. They don't grind, they allow. It's a feeling of pure presence. How do athletes do it? Well, guess what? They don't have to do anything!

That's right, once someone believes that they have to do something to get it, they're lost before they begin because there is no action required. I know for myself, playing squash at first team level, that when I am in the zone, everything seems calm and still. It feels like I am walking on air and I don't need to try to do anything. Moving seems effortless. Hitting winning shots feels like I am not even doing it myself. There is something quite magical about it.

Take it from the top

Apart from giving their athletes a complete understanding of how the whole process works, let's look at what else the coaches and trainers *can* do.

As I have said time and again in this book, what you say is far less important that the state of mind you're in when you say it (unless you are fully aware of the process at the time). This is true in every relationship, and especially that of a coach and athlete. Let me give you an example.

I am a huge football fan, and follow a team in England by the name of Arsenal. Don't hold it against me, it's been in the family for generations now. My Grandfather took Grandma on their first date to watch them, and my dad had trials with them way back in the 60s. The current coach of Arsenal is a Frenchman by the name of Arsène Wenger. He is a studious character and is well known for his half time team talks. One of the players under his tutelage, when Arsenal went a whole season unbeaten (which is a record that may never be equalled) was Ray Parlour.

Ray went onto play for a number of other clubs before he retired. One day on a radio show called 'TalkSport' I heard him reflecting on his career and he said something very interesting. He was talking about his times at Arsenal and how Arsène would get the players ready for the second half during the half time break. The interviewer asked Ray at one point *"What was it about Arsène's team talks that was so different from the others you used to hear?"* *"Nothing"* said Ray. *"At least not in the content. He just calmly and clearly explained to us what we needed to do and how we needed to do it. The only difference was that the others (managers) were usually shouting at us!"* Of course the net result was, that Arsenal went onto win most of their matches in the second half. I can't say the same for any of Ray's other teams...

Arsène did not force his ideas or beliefs on his players. He got them to see for themselves the relevance and intelligence behind them. As Syd Banks said: *"If you take a belief of your own and replace it with another's belief, you might experience a temporary placebo effect, but you have not found a lasting answer. However, if a person replaces an old belief with a realisation from his or her own wisdom, the effect and results are superior and permanent."*

The net result of this for Arsenal (who were nicknamed the 'Invincibles' for that season), was that the players trusted the manager. He did not need to shout and bellow at them. They knew that by listening to him, they would get the necessary advice that they required; that it would feel right for them inside and that it would ultimately be the right course of action. For a whole season at least, that proved to be the case!

Engagement cannot be commanded. It has to occur at an individual level. The coach's role as a leader therefore lies in his or her ability to show each individual that they have the ability themselves to be motivated, or collectively as a team. They have to be able to assist the player to access their own inner wisdom and guidance.

Another point to make here is about the state of mind of the players who are receiving the team talk. If they are behind at half time, they might be caught up in their own extraneous thinking about their performance. Arsène's calm and assured approach was more effective than shouting at them would have been. If the players are caught up in their own thinking, it would be better to help them access their own wisdom and clarity through calmness, not aggression. Shouting at them would simply compound their feelings of shame and if their level of consciousness descended further, effort and performance would probably follow.

It's a trick of the mind...

I touched on the fact earlier that experts believe that it is the performance of the athlete that affects his or her mental state, but this cannot be the case. The truth is that an athlete's insecure thoughts will <u>never</u> originate from his or her form. It looks like it, but it's simply not the case.

Once again, the missing link here is thought, and the misunderstanding of the process of how thought is created leads to this basic misunderstanding of what 'form' really is. So many athletes fall into the trap of thinking that when form is constant, rituals and processes need to stay the same, but if performance suffers – change them all!

The problem of form therefore is not a problem at all! What they fail to see is that there is no such thing as 'problems', per se. A problem is merely 'another view'. In fact in Arabic, this is the direct translation of the word. It is an opportunity to see things differently. <u>If we did not have problems, we would not grow</u>. When players have a deeper understanding of the Principles behind their thought processes, they are more aware of this. They don't see 'missed shots' or 'lost games', they see potential to uncover the meaning of the performance and the challenge ahead.

Likewise, good form or a win should feel the same and not be ruled by the ego's willingness to take over and bask in the glory! This is where major pitfalls await for the unsuspecting athlete. Taking this feeling and making it the reason for their happiness is a rocky road to ruin. That's not where happiness lies. It lies *within* us all, not as a *result* of an outside event.

How many times have we heard one of our sporting heroes finding relief in a quick fix from the outside world to try to emulate the feeling of success that their careers brought to them (or so they thought)? They soon discover that those feelings too, were short lived. The list of fallen sports stars who turned to drink and drugs, gambling and promiscuous sex goes on and on and will continue to do so, as long as we maintain the belief that happiness comes from anything outside of ourselves.

When we act on thought, trying to suppress or replace it, we get into trouble. When we trust our thoughts as our reality, purely out of a poor state of mind, we get into trouble too. A really good example of this is if you have ever acted upon an urge to do something with a hangover. I know I used to, and I went on to regret it. My state of mind was low and my thinking way, way off-base, but I trusted the feeling. Wrong! As we know, thought is the link between the outside world – what is happening out there – and our inner world. It is the quality of our thinking, and having an understanding of where thought originates that is key, not the thoughts themselves.

In sport then, we can feel amazing about a win and attribute it to good performance, team work and practice. In contrast, a poor performance is usually attributed to circumstances, low quality of mind or dip in form, but rarely to coming up against better opposition who you can learn from. It all depends on your own understanding of the process – I've known people who've won tournaments and still been utterly miserable, so there's no hard and fast rule, other than having an understanding of thought!

Let's bring this back to you for a moment. You know the feeling, one day you think your partner is the best thing ever, the next you are seeing their every fault magnified. It's your own thinking that's the key, not them! Our realities are created by our own thoughts, not by the world around us. Just having this knowledge means that instead of looking narrowly at a situation and thinking that it is our own personal problem, see it for what is it: thought! Perhaps there is a potential for change – but see what else can be done instead first. Allow the murky waters to settle and clarity of mind to come back before you decide.

I would suggest that being aware of your feelings is important here. Your feelings are a very good indicator. If they feel tight, then proceed with caution. Don't take *the thinking* too seriously. If your feelings are calm and relaxed, you can be more trusting of the thinking. The best thing about a negative feeling is that it strongly encourages us to reassess the direction in which you are heading. Any life situation combined with an insecure state of mind however may create the false impression of a problem, resulting in worry or stress. Once we see where this thinking originates from, we realise that the worst thing to do is look outside of ourselves for a fix.

Your happiness is not dependant on your circumstances, no matter what it looks like at any given moment. As Eckhart Tolle says: *"You can always improve your life situation, but you can never improve your life."* Life doesn't happen to us, it just happens. Whatever value we assign to any given event, is what we choose to assign to it at that moment. Being turned down for a date = bad. Scoring the winning goal = good. Although we can play a part in the circumstance, life itself carries on unbiased, regardless.

If we perform any task with an outcome attached to the end result, it's a surefire way to narrow the perceptive field. We are limiting our options. Our expectations of contentment or otherwise, divert our attention away from the task at hand. Once we can see this for ourselves and realise it at a deeper level, it will give us the freedom that allows us to be more productive. Anything is possible!

Goal setting therefore, especially in sports, is not a good plan of action. Daniel H Pink in his book on motivation; 'Drive' found that workers become more imaginative and efficient at performing tasks if there is no reward on the outcome. When we focus on a prize, the options narrow. Having a goal 'to win' is one thing (and is to be applauded), but having that goal as the reason for your happiness, is not!

We don't see things as they are... we see them as we are — Anais Nin

Roberto de Vicenzo, the famous Argentine golfer, once won a tournament, and after receiving the cheque and smiling for the cameras, he went to the clubhouse and prepared to leave. Sometime later he walked alone to his car in the parking lot and was approached by a young woman. She congratulated him on his victory and then told him that her child was seriously ill and near death.

De Vicenzo was touched by her story and took out a pen and endorsed his winning payment to the woman. "Make some good days for the baby," he said as he pressed the cheque into her hand.

The next week he was having lunch in a country club when a PGA official came to his table. "Some of the guys in the parking lot last week told me you met a young woman there after you won the tournament".

De Vicenzo nodded. "Well", said the official, "I have news for you. She's a phony. She's not married. She has no sick baby. She fleeced you, my friend".'

"You mean there is no baby who is dying?" said de Vicenzo.
"That's right".'
"That's the best news I've heard all week!"'

The first time I read this, I was on a train going into London which had been severely delayed. I immediately began to see things differently. I looked around at the people in the carriage and saw a young woman with two children who were in a state of sheer bliss at being stuck on the train. My mood changed at that very moment. Nothing about the situation changed, only my thinking about it. When we live life from the inside-out, it becomes easier to act in harmony with life and to go with the flow.

Now Roberto De Vicenzo had probably never heard of the Principles before. Nor for that matter have quite a few people who live their lives from the inside out. Knowing about them does not take away from the fact that every single one of us on this planet *uses them* from day-to-day. It's not about knowing what they are, it's about understanding how the system works which gives you the freedom to make choices such as Roberto's.

Life can be good or bad, painful or painless, but it's *always* up to you. Knowing this is how it works through these Principles, is just a nudge in the right direction. That's all. No more, no less. No magic bullet, just an understanding of the process.

Roberto had this guidance from whatever source. My partner Victoria, had no idea what the Principles were and lives her life in the same manner. She got her own insights from life and made her own choices. Hearing about the Principles, was like hearing about something that she already knew and had seen deeply already. It was just a confirmation for her of an inner truth.

Living a life without a narrow view of what is possible gives you freedom. Showing this to our children gives them their own freedom to make choices, especially when it comes to playing competitive sports. My own daughter loves winning. She gets that from her mother, and who am I to say this is 'wrong'? But she doesn't think it's the end of the world if she comes second either. Third maybe, but not second!

When our thoughts and feelings go astray, we feel the need to come up with a solution and this includes in the sporting arena. I hope that I have shown you in this chapter, that no matter what the circumstance, or the field of play, often the best approach is to do nothing in that moment and allow our psychological functioning to return to normal.

Your state of mind is the source of experience, not the effect. Your relationship to your thoughts and not the circumstances is the key to help you deal with anything that confronts you, including sporting challenges.

Chapter Nine

Money

"Not everything that counts can be counted, and not everything that can be counted counts" – Albert Einstein

Everybody thinks about money differently. Some rich people are happy, some are unhappy. Some poor people are happy, some aren't. Famous people all over the world with serious substance abuse and emotional problems demonstrate that fame and fortune are not always the route to happiness.

Michael Neill in his book '*Supercoach*' tells us about a client of his with a net worth of six hundred million dollars, who woke up every morning wondering 'Is this the day I'm going to lose it all'? You would think that with that amount of money, you would have enough to keep anybody happy, right...? Might I suggest that if you think that money is going to 'make you' happy, you are looking in the wrong place for the good feelings. Your well being is not dependent on your bank balance!

On my own journey of discovering this, I have had many ups and downs along the way. I remember once, I made my last (and I mean last) twenty pounds stretch a whole two weeks. Travel, food, drink, everything. It was an amazing feeling to achieve it. What was most amazing though, was the experiences that I got out of those two weeks of financial discipline. Instead of driving the car to a networking event or a meeting, I walked. I made more time –

and I walked. I took in the crisp autumn air as I meandered down roads that I would never have driven down and noticed things in the minutest detail. I had time to think, but also the time to let my thinking go.

Some of the best choices and decisions I have ever made in my life came from those two weeks when I had but twenty pounds to my name. Having the space to just 'be' and the time to let my inner wisdom rise to the surface was literally life changing. Yet I had only twenty quid left to live on. Did I worry? On occasions, my clouds of negative thinking returned and I started to get fooled by the illusion. But I soon remembered that it wasn't real. "*The very persistent reality*" as Einstein called it, returned now and again. But I did nothing (worry-wise), and it went away.

What is also amazing is that the thinking that could have clouded my experience would not have got me the results that my lack of thinking did! The inner wisdom and ideas that came to me in those moments walking outside are actually part of what you are reading right now. The idea for this book came from those two weeks of thoughtless poverty!

It's no fluke that a lot of people I speak to about this say similar things: "*My moments of greatest clarity came when I had nothing left, when I let go*". The circumstances may change slightly, but having the opportunity to just let go seems to work magnificently.

There is a wonderful video on YouTube called 'Surrender', in which Oprah Winfrey describes the moment that she read a review in the *New York Times* about a new book called '*The Colour Purple*' by Alice Walker. It resonated so strongly with her that she immediately put a dressing gown over her pyjamas and went straight to the mall. She started reading the book right there in the store and finished it that very day. She went back that night before the bookstore closed and bought the rest of the copies on the shelf and started to give them to everyone that she knew.

At the time, Steven Spielberg and Quincy Jones were making a movie of the book. Oprah made a pledge to be 'in that movie'. She found an audition and went along. Now Oprah was a totally unknown actress then, so months later and still not hearing anything, she called the casting agent to ask about how the audition went. *"You don't call us, we call you!"* they said. *"We have REAL actresses auditioning for this part, Alfre Woodard has just left my office, she's a real actress, you have no experience."*

Believing that she had not got the part because she was too fat, Oprah went to a health farm to lose some weight. She had believed, I mean really believed in her heart of hearts, that she was meant to be in *that* film. So whilst running around an athletics track on a cold rainy day, she wanted to thank God for giving her the opportunity for at least trying out for the part... but it was too hard. She had to let it go, but it was too hard, just *too* hard. And then a song just spontaneously came to her and she started singing *"I surrender, I surrender all. All to thee my blessed Saviour, I surrender all"*. At first, she was just singing it, but then she started to feel it, really feel it. She started to cry as she sang and then she felt herself really 'let it go'.

At that point, she knew... knew from the depth of her heart that she would be 'alright'. At first she thought, 'I'll be alright, but I'll never be able to see the movie'. Then she thought, 'I'll be alright, I'll be able to see the movie and bless the actors and actresses in that movie, and I'll be able to say *"It's a good thing you got the part..."* I'll be able to do that'. Then she saw herself actually watching the movie and being OK. 'My life will go on and I will not be bitter and I will not be angry and I will not hold it and feel it for the rest of my life and say "She got the part, and I didn't". I will have peace...'

And in the moment it happened to her, in that exact moment, somebody came running out to the track and said "There's a phone call for you". It was Steven Spielberg. He said "I hear you're at a fat farm? If you drop one more pound, you'll lose the part!"

What is the point of these stories? What have these got to do with money? In both cases, mine and Oprah's, a real turning point in our lives happened when there was nothing left. In those moments of 'emptiness', real life had the space to flow right in.

And yet, most of us see these moments in a completely different way. Our thinking tells us that it is an emergency, a disaster! We attach all sorts of outcomes to the meaning or worse still, we make up meanings that don't even exist and attach outcomes to those.

"OK", I hear you say... "I get you: moments of clarity, emptiness, space – but what the hell has that got to do with me paying my mortgage?"

Alright, so let's say that the money is running out, the business is on a slippery slope and the house, car and marriage are at risk. Big enough for you? Let's say that you are obsessed with this problem. It would be easy to think that the difficulty of this problem is the cause of your obsession with it. You lay awake at night worrying about it, and the consequences of not solving it. The truth is, at the level of understanding that you have about this problem, there is no solution.

You can't solve problems by using the same kind of thinking you used when you created them. When you try to grind away at a problem, and you do not have the understanding to solve it at that level, try letting go of your current obsession with that problem and see what happens. Think of it as throwing the sand bags off the balloon to make it float up higher. In terms of thought and your thinking about it, do nothing!

The heavy unpleasant negative feeling is not real, you made it up. The scene in your head is not real, that's your creation too. If you went for a walk, the second you got some distance from the problem, the whole scene would change. The feelings would change. The scene you see would feel better than the scene you saw before. You might find answers that you did not have before.

Here's a real life example taken from one of George Pransky's clients in New York. In fact, this was the guy who actually had the problems that I outlined above. He was in way over his head financially. He had defaulted on the mortgage and he hadn't been filing his taxes either, so the IRS was after him, as well as everything else. George knew that all he had to do was to raise this guy's level of understanding about how thought was created and answers to (seemingly) unsolvable problems would eventually come. And they did. After this happened, he told George the following: *"You know, George, I can't believe how lucky I am. I've lived twenty years above my means, under pressure, worried every night... and now I have the chance to completely rectify that by declaring bankruptcy or set up payment plans that I can actually fulfil. I lived with a ghost in my head about the doorbell ringing any moment from the IRS. I have nothing weighing on me anymore. You told me I was looking at a painful and unpleasant mirage and I already have the answers within me. I can now see my life in a hopeful way. I have the answers, I can start over again.*

I'm going to lose this house, but to tell you the truth, this house was ill-gotten gains anyway. My wife and I, who have both been living under the pressure of it all for years, now have a chance of a totally fresh start together. We're never going to go back to how it was. The lesson has been learned. This has been the best thing that ever happened to us, it's a new beginning."

Powerful stuff, eh?

I'll give you another example. I have a friend who lives in Greece. At the time of writing, there is total turmoil on the money markets regarding the Eurozone. Banks who have loaned a great deal of money to countries who can't afford to pay it are in danger of losing their investment. In very real terms, this means that the people affected by the crisis will be the general public. Hundreds of thousands, if not millions, of jobs will be lost. Companies will go bankrupt, there will be 'runs' on the bank and a great deal of social unrest.

My friend is really, really worried about this. His wife wants to leave the country. His parents want to do the same. But his children ask questions like, *"Daddy, does that mean we will have to live in a tent. Can we please live in a tent?"* And *"Will we have to grow all of our own food, because we love to do that?"* And *"So that means that school will be closed too".*

Do you see a difference here? Children, in their naturally curious, wonderful, excited and adventurous state see the possibilities of it all. Adults see the problems. But remember what 'problems' are? A different view.

How different life would be if we looked at things as if we were all children again. My friend and his wife currently give their children home tutoring, grow their own food and live in rented accommodation, which means that they can move quickly and easily. They spend a lot more time together as a consequence and can live pretty much anywhere they want. The economy has still gone south, but they're happier than they ever were before.

So you can see, even in the worst and most dire circumstances, the answers are still there, even though it looks like they're not. As your level of understanding goes up, you see a different world.

Now that you can see how it is possible to look at any situation in a new light, let's look at quality of mind when it comes to making decisions about money, because we know where that can lead without an understanding of what's really going on!

If you read through Napoleon Hill's book '*Think And Grow Rich*', (the title of which should really read: '*Don't Think, Let Your Wisdom Come Through And Do The Thinking For You, And Then Grow Rich*'), you will find that there is a lot of emphasis on 'doing'. So it's no great surprise that this particular book does not help the majority of its readers. The same goes for '*The Secret*' and '*The Science Of Getting Rich*'. The call to 'focus on your goal as if it were a reality' is treading in dangerous territory. For starters, we are making the assumption that money makes you happy, which it doesn't. It looks like it, but it doesn't. Secondly, it's certainly true that you get what you focus on, but so many people (already in dire financial circumstances) try to get into a 'positive state of mind', hold it there for a while, then start thinking about debt again and the thought shatters. They end up focussing on the debt, not the wealth. Again, they are focussing on debt as a 'bad' thing, which is reinforcing the idea that wealth is a 'good' thing. That's looking in the wrong direction.

Let's focus on the task in hand here. We want to be able to make 'wise' decisions about money. If you now go and ask those people to make decisions about money in their desperate state, they will struggle, as their *thinking* is off-base. Try getting someone who thinks that their well being depends on a sale to do a negotiation for you. They'll take the first sensible offer on the table and sometimes just the first offer, period. Which is why pawn shops do a roaring trade in recessions!

The way we see money, the way we feel about money and what money *actually is,* seems a bit skewed really. So here's what I think about money: money is a tool which allows us to do stuff. There is plenty of it to go around and plenty of it out there. In fact, any place where there is a positive difference to be made, there is money to be made.

How you see money, is how it is for you, however that might be. If you think it's scary, then it's scary. If you think it's easy to come by, it'll be easy to come by. If you wonder why you never have enough, you'll never have enough. Why? Because it's all about the *thinking about the money,* not the money itself. If you think that having more money will make you happy, your mind is playing a trick on you. You might feel better for a little while, but that feeling will go because the thought behind it remains. *"Just two more grand, and I'll be happy".*

Really, I'm telling you now, you don't even need it. You might think you do, but you don't. I was involved on a discussion on one of the TED forums recently entitled: *'If you had $10 trillion, what would you do with it?'* There were some pretty interesting (and pretty silly) points being made in the discussion, but I stirred it up a bit by adding the following: *"If a meteorite hit the other side of the planet tomorrow, wiping out all of the financial systems on the planet, what would you then spend the $10 trillion on?"*

What followed was a complete turn-around in the conversation to what was important to people. It was all about family and survival and self sufficiency. The money systems of the world aren't even *real*! They only exist on a digital level. There's not actually a real 'stash of cash' sitting in a large warehouse somewhere.

The true value in things lies within your own thinking about them. Nothing more, nothing less. Give money to an Amazon tribesman and he'll use it for kindling. Money is as real as you want to make it. The value of money is as real as you want to make it. And how you make it, is up to you. I know very talented people who are out of work and very stupid people who are highly-paid. There's no hard and fast rule to any of it, only that which you make up yourself.

However, if you spend more time working on yourself – your energy, your ability to serve and give to others – your well being will come right along with you. I'm fairly sure that financial abundance will follow (although you might not really care about it so much by then). It happened for me like this, along with countless others and I'm sure you'll be no different. I do what I love and the recompense always seems to follow. There's just a natural flow to it.

What I want you to get to grips with here is: don't fret about money. Don't even think about it! Just be who you are meant to be and fulfil your own destiny, and the rest will follow. If you really, really want to create money, the only thing getting in your way is thought. So stop thinking about it and go create!

Chapter Ten

The Principles in everyday life

"A human being is a part of a whole, called by us 'universe', a part limited in time and space. He experiences himself, his thoughts and feelings as something separated from the rest... a kind of optical delusion of his consciousness. This delusion is a kind of prison for us, restricting us to our personal desires and to affection for a few persons nearest to us. Our task must be to free ourselves from this prison by widening our circle of compassion to embrace all living creatures and the whole of nature in its beauty" – Albert Einstein

So what next? Well I thought I would add a chapter at the end of the book as a general discussion on what having an understanding of the Principles means in everyday life for me personally and for those around me.

I had originally planned to call this chapter: 'The Principles as a Way of Life', but realised this would not be appropriate. The Principles are <u>not</u> a way to life, they are simply *an explanation for how life works*, a description of how life happens for us. They are not a means to live a happy life. They are not a tool or a technique, or an answer or anything else of the sort. They are simply there and we can recognise through them the way the system works and essentially, how the 'trick' is done.

Does a knowledge of the Principles stop bad things happening? Absolutely not. But having this understanding will put us in a position of strength, in the same way that having an understanding of how machines work or cars run or computers operate, helps us.

If we understand what is really going on, we will simply not suffer so much, because the suffering is only self-created.

Living with an understanding of the Principles brings with it incredible freedom. I can still get so close to my thinking that I just don't see the wood for the trees, so to speak, but I don't get fooled as often as I used to. When I do, I just see it more quickly and I know what's going on now.

With an understanding of the Principles, we have a new frame of reference composed of deeper wisdom, better judgement and more happiness. As Syd said: *"The Three Principles enable us to acknowledge and respond to existence."* They are always operating. Although they are invisible, the way they work together at any given moment determines the form that each person's reality takes. But let's get something straight here. The Principles are explanatory and not prescriptive. They are an explanation of the human operating system. Nothing more... nothing less. So let me do a quick recap once again, just to leave it fresh in your mind: Our experience is generated from the inside-out via the workings of the Three Principles of Mind, Thought and Consciousness. Everyone has the ability to interpret the results of this process through their own freewill. Everyone creates their own picture of life, their reality, through the gift of thought.

Just having an understanding that this is how the system works is enough to give a person freedom from tunnelled thought. Realise how the system works and accept that this is how it is. The raising in your level of consciousness will be enough to keep you from putting misplaced belief in off-base thinking. We are then able to recognise the experience more fully when it happens, and see when we are getting lost in the illusion.

We can see how our own innate wisdom can get buried beneath our own thinking and previously held beliefs, and why it seems like (at the time) this wisdom could never be recovered. We don't have to try and replace this thinking with more positive thinking or change our thoughts – this will only create anxiety and stress, especially if it is unsuccessful. We don't do anything at all, we simply let the next thinking roll on in like the waves on the ocean and return to our natural state of calm. We see that it is only our personal thinking that is preventing this from happening.

Every feeling, emotion and behaviour that has and will ever occur, can be explained via the Three Principles. There are no exceptions. *Mind, Thought and Consciousness create the contents of our world and have done since day one.* When we form a thought, that thought seems real for us. How things look, how we feel and what we do, are the effects of Thought. Thought is the ability to create images in our heads and the Three Principles work together to make these images a reality for us. As long as we are alive and conscious, this is how it works. <u>Feelings and emotions are a reflection of the way we experience our thoughts</u>. As Syd pointed out: *"Our feelings are a barometer of our thought. When the mind is filled with positive thoughts, cause and effect rule."*

If you hear a fire alarm going off in a building, you know that it's time to leave. If you put your hand into a flame, you get told by your body exactly what to do. So it is with our emotions. If we feel tension, anger and worry, it's time to not trust our thinking at that moment. Yet we tend to do the opposite. We steam into things, just like we would be racing back into that burning building or putting our hand back into that flame! When we understand this distinction and know that these are the warning signs, we are starting to understand the role of thought in our lives. <u>When we believe that our thoughts come as a result of our feelings, we are being lost in the illusion of life</u>. That's when people see circumstances as the cause of their ills. Even though we feel that we have legitimate, compelling reasons for feeling this, it is still us generating this feeling <u>via</u> thought, interfering with our natural wisdom and well being in the process. <u>*We are always feeling our thinking, no exceptions*</u>.

When we begin to see this more in our day-to-day lives and spot the times when we are getting fooled by our own thoughts, we take things less personally. We see that people do what feels right to them at that time – what serves them best and makes sense to them at that moment, and most of the time, people's behaviour has nothing to do with 'us' at all. People do what they do because they feel that it is their best or only choice, *given their thinking in that moment*. If we can see this for ourselves, we are usually in a better position to help the other person calm down and get back to their own wisdom and common sense. After all, it's harder to help anyone if we take a critical or judgemental view on them. That is only seeing it from our own perspective. Yes, it may seem wrong to us but it's not <u>us</u> that's seeing it that way.

Another reason for taking a sympathetic approach is that when a person is challenged on their behaviour, they tend to become defensive (remember the children in the Parenting chapter). However, when people see their own psychological innocence in what they do, they are able to forgive themselves more easily, rather than getting caught up in guilt and the feelings attached to it, which would take them deeper down into the spiral.

I recently finished working for the charity 'Crisis at Christmas'. It is a homeless charity offering food, shelter, advice, and friendship (amongst other things) to homeless people for ten days over the festive period. It does so much more than this throughout the year, but I won't go into that here. Suffice to say that it is an excellent charity that has been saving and changing lives now for nearly forty years.

This year, I volunteered at the dependency centre in Central London. It is the only shelter where 'guests', as they are known, are allowed to drink alcohol. They are not officially allowed to take drugs there, although some still do. One of the reasons that Crisis has been so successful as a charity over the years is that it manages to get homeless people into their own accommodation during this Christmas period. Whilst in the shelters, it encourages the guests to do activities other than drinking. They get lots of time to talk to the volunteers and share their stories. Above all else, they are listened to. This safe and secure environment is key, because people feel better about themselves when they feel safe and secure. And when they feel better about themselves, they make better decisions (like how and where they can get somewhere to live!) In short, people change when they feel better. When they are not so up against it, they are able to consider new possibilities.

As a result of this year's efforts, there were 673 advice sessions given, 629 healthcare appointments, five guests found alternatives to rough sleeping and another five entered detox. Everyone's innate health and inner wisdom is ultimately buoyant (like the beachball being held under water). When people hit rock bottom, like the vagrants at Crisis this year, they stop defending or trusting their current thinking. It simply has not worked for them, and now they have the proof.

One of the tasks for the volunteers, of which there are thousands every year, is to keep an eye on the guests in the sleeping areas. These are rough sleepers, so they tend to keep all of their possessions close to them. If they go to the toilet, which is a luxury for them, they can be quite touchy leaving their belongings for even a moment. So the volunteers keep an eye out for them and make sure that they remain safe. It is at this point in the evening that the volunteers have a chance to catch up on some reading whilst keeping an eye on the guests. And so it was that I was reading 'Wisdom for Life' by the late Dr Roger Mills and the lovely Elsie Spittle.

In one chapter, Roger was talking about his work with dependency clients and made an interesting point, that most errant behaviour boils down to one thing: insecurity – which I touched upon earlier in the chapter on Parenting. Because insecurity originates in our own learned thoughts.

Self destructive, negative thinking looks real and contaminates our everyday experience of life. We take it with us to the next stop on our journey and we let it affect us. If we are told that we are useless, we take that belief with us. But if we see this is just thought, and we realise via an insight that this is just an insecure 'habit of thought', we are able to see the connection between this thinking and our current behaviour and essentially do nothing with it.

But what about these people's history of abuse and neglect? What about the so-called reasons that got them into this mess? Thinking about the past in a certain way and not the past itself is the real problem. Memories are not to be forgotten, however we can always look at them from a new vantage point and get a different perspective. We can experience insights which will piece them together in a different way. We can learn from the past or keep repeating the past, depending on the perspective from which we view it.

In my opinion, one of the reasons that so many damaged people turn to drink and drugs is that they cannot tolerate their own thoughts, because these thoughts are so negative and hopeless. So they numb themselves to stop having to deal with them at all. They live in an unfeeling reality, devoid of hope. Their thoughts create a living hell for them, then they fight that thinking every day with their behaviours. But, no matter how depressed or angry or paranoid or cynical they feel at that moment, there have always been times in that person's life, even if it was only for a fleeting second, where sanity, well being and common sense prevailed. Yet the field of prevention often focuses on the *errant* behaviour. It should be focussing on the potential for this healthy behaviour to re-emerge. If they had it once, they are capable of having it again – because this is where the healing lies! It is only a habit of thinking that is keeping this reality alive for them. They say that there is no way to stop this kind of thinking, that it is too powerful to control and too compelling to get out of their heads. The answer would be to stop trying – do nothing! Trying will only lead to the downward spiral of failure and self defeat that we discussed earlier.

There really is nothing to do. Recognise the thinking, accept it for what it is and wait for the next thinking to come along and replace it. No matter how bad things look, new thinking will always arrive sooner or later and replace it.

As Dr Roger Mills said: *"One of the most exciting things we can realise as human beings is that the mind is designed to function in a healthy way. We interfere with that process with insecure thinking"*.

People build an inner world – a reality that looks very real to them, even though it is made up entirely of thought. This looks so real to them that they take up residency there. When these thoughts are seen for what they are; habits of thinking that tend to build on themselves, they are no longer a factor. No one's mind is limited to producing negative thoughts and once people quiet their turbulent thinking, they find common sense, clear thinking and insight.

So you see, people are at the mercy of the ebb and flow of their own thinking until they see how the system works through the Three Principles. They see other people as the ones responsible for *making them* unhappy or angry and this thinking can sometimes lead to violence or abuse. When you have an understanding of the Principles, it allows you to see the illusion and to then tap into your own common sense and feel more loving and secure. There is also a freshness and vitality to this wisdom that allows you to keep an open mind and learn new things. You are able to maintain your calm and well being irrespective of your situation, if you know how this works.

For example, training in the Principles for police officers in some areas in the US helped them see that they could get more cooperation from citizens if they treated them with more respect. This involved seeing beyond their own thinking and conditioned habits of responding, to how the situation looked from the other person's perspective. They were then able to respond in a firm manner that commanded respect rather than adding fuel to the fire.

When we get to the higher ground of common sense and wisdom, we must show others how to get there by example, instead of jumping back into taking things personally and reacting out of ego and blame (running back into the burning building). *Wisdom produces understanding.* This is the solvent that cuts through the thought-created barriers of prejudice, hatred and discord. With it, we can recognise our common humanity.

When people malign those from other cultures, they are holding onto injustices and resentments from the past. People rarely act with malicious intent, although it may look like that from our perspective if we take things personally. They act from within their own thought-created world of their own reality. They are doing what they feel they need to do to serve their own best interests at the time. They begin to discover the deeper wisdom within them, they cannot imagine why those thoughts made sense or seemed meaningful before. Because, (I believe) no one is inherently evil. People do evil things, but they do so because it makes sense to them at the time, for whatever reason. The feelings and behaviours that look that way to them are learned. We are taught to hate and fear and to attack when we feel threatened. But as Ghandi and Martin Luther King showed, we get a lot further with wisdom.

We need to be able to trust and explore the unknown in ourselves; to be willing to drop the learned habits of thought about ourselves and others. If we put aside our separate realities, we can work together to solve common problems as a global community.

As we begin to understand the workings of the universe more, we are seeing that the forces behind the physical are microscopic and invisible. When we look beneath the contents of our current thinking and habits of thought, we see the fabric that produces reality before form.

Universal intelligence exists inside and outside of our bodies.

It is in everything and everyone. We are always immersed in this intelligence, whether we realise it or not. As Syd said: *"True wisdom is not discovered, but uncovered from an uncontaminated innate intelligence. Wisdom lies beyond our delusionary ego and personal thought system. Believe me, words do not convey the magnificence of the hidden treasures that lie within."*

Words are simply the medium that I have had to use within this book to convey the ideas that they hold. They are not the ideas themselves. They merely point towards what is true and only you can see that for yourself.

I hope that I have given you a taste of what is possible in your life with an understanding of the Principles. But it's like art – not everybody is going to feel it and you can't make them. However, you can show them some important pieces and maybe they'll fall in love. I hope I have done this for you within these pages.

And ultimately? Well everybody wants to feel more connected in life. People think that control is the answer but actually, letting go of control is the key. Have faith that we are all fine without all of that 'other stuff'. There's well being inside of us already and there's nothing to do to get it. We are already perfect, there is nowhere to go. We already have all the answers.

Simply point yourself in the right direction and DO NOTHING!

Appendix

Ram Dass Gives Maharaji the 'Yogi Medicine'

by Ram Dass

In 1967 when I first came to India, I brought with me a supply of LSD, hoping to find someone who might understand more about these substances than we did in the West.

When I had met Maharaji (Neem Karoli Baba), after some days the thought had crossed my mind that he would be a perfect person to ask. The next day after having that thought, I was called to him and he asked me immediately, "Do you have a question?"

Of course, being before him was such a powerful experience that I had completely forgotten the question I had had in my mind the night before. So I looked stupid and said, "No, Maharajji, I have no question." He appeared irritated and said, "Where is the medicine?"

I was confused but Bhagavan Dass suggested, "Maybe he means the LSD?" I asked and Maharajji nodded. The bottle of LSD was in the car and I was sent to fetch it. When I returned I emptied the vile of pills into my hand. In addition to the LSD there were a number of other pills for this and that – diarrhoea, fever, a sleeping pill, and so forth. He asked about each of these.

He asked if they gave powers. I didn't understand at the time and thought that by 'powers' perhaps he meant physical strength. I said, "No." Later, of course, I came to understand that the word he had used, "siddhis," means psychic powers.

Then he held out his hand for the LSD. I put one pill on his palm. Each of these pills was about three hundred micrograms of very pure LSD – a solid dose for an adult. He beckoned for more, so I put a second pill in his hand – six hundred micrograms. Again he beckoned and I added yet another, making the total dosage nine hundred micrograms – certainly not a dose for beginners. Then he threw all the pills into his mouth. My reaction was one of shock mixed with fascination of a social scientist eager to see what would happen.

He allowed me to stay for an hour – and nothing happened. Nothing whatsoever. He just laughed at me.

The whole thing had happened very fast and unexpectedly. When I returned to the United States in 1968 I told many people about this acid feat. But there had remained in me a gnawing doubt that perhaps he had been putting me on and had thrown the pills over his shoulder or palmed them, because I hadn't actually seen them go into his mouth.

Three years later, when I was back in India, he asked me one day, "Did you give me medicine when you were in India last time?"

"Yes."

"Did I take it?" he asked. (Ah, there was my doubt made manifest!)

"I think you did."

"What happened?

"Nothing."

"Oh! Jao!" and he sent me off for the evening.

The next morning I was called over to the porch in front of his room, where he sat in the mornings on a tucket. He asked, "Have you got any more of that medicine?"

It just so happened that I was carrying a small supply of LSD for 'just in case,' and this was obviously it. "Yes."

"Get it," he said.

So I did. In the bottle were five pills of three hundred micrograms each. One of the pills was broken. I placed them on my palm and held them out to him. He took the four unbroken pills. Then, one by one, very obviously and very deliberately, he placed each one in his mouth and swallowed it – another unspoken thought of mine now answered.

As soon as he had swallowed the last one, he asked, "Can I take water?"

"Yes."

"Hot or cold?"

"It doesn't matter."

He started yelling for water and drank a cup when it was brought.

Then he asked," How long will it take to act?"

"Anywhere from twenty minutes to an hour."

He called for an older man, a long-time devotee who had a watch, and Maharajji held the man's wrist, often pulling it up to him to peer at the watch.

Then he asked, "Will it make me crazy?"

That seemed so bizarre to me that I could only go along with what seemed to be a gag.

So I said, "Probably."

And then we waited. After some time he pulled the blanket over his face, and when he came out after a moment his eyes were rolling and his mouth was ajar and he looked totally mad. I got upset.

What was happening? Had I misjudged his powers? After all, he was an old man (though how old I had no idea), and I had let him take twelve hundred micrograms. Maybe last time he had thrown them away and then he read my mind and was trying to prove to me he could do it, not realizing how strong the 'medicine' really was. Guilt and anxiety poured through me. But when I looked at him again he was perfectly normal and looking at the watch.

At the end of an hour it was obvious nothing had happened. His reactions had been a total put-on. And then he asked, "Have you got anything stronger?" I didn't. Then he said, "These medicines were used in Kulu Valley long ago. But yogis have lost that knowledge. They were used with fasting. Nobody knows now. To take them with no effect, your mind must be firmly fixed on God. Others would be afraid to take. Many saints would not take this." And he left it at that.

When I asked him if I should take LSD again, he said, "It should not be taken in a hot climate. If you are in a place that is cool and peaceful, and you are alone and your mind is turned toward God, then you may take the yogi medicine."

Be connected
(or how to further your understanding of the Principles)

In my opinion, the very best resource for understanding the Principles is the original work of Syd Banks, however there are many other sources now available as well as his wonderful books:

Print

The Enlightened Gardener by Syd Banks

The Missing Link by Syd Banks

Second Chance by Syd Banks

Dear Liza by Syd Banks

The Enlightened Gardener Revisited by Syd Banks

The Quest of the Pearl: A Novel by Syd Banks

Somebody Should Have Told Us! by Jack Pransky

The Relationship Handbook by George Pransky

Wisdom for Life: The Principles for Well-Being by Elsie Spittle

Our True Identity...Three Principles by Elsie Spittle

Supercoach: 10 Secrets to Transform Anyone's Life by Michael Neill

The Spark Inside by Ami Chen Mills-Naim

Parenting from the Heart: A Guide to the Essence of Parenting by Jack Pransky

Modello: A Story of Hope for the Inner City and Beyond by Jack Pransky

Stillpower: The Inner Source of Athletic Excellence by Garret Kramer

The Wisdom Within by Dr Roger Mills & Elsie Spittle

Awareness by Anthony De Mello

Synchronicity: The Inner Path of Leadership by Joseph Jaworski

The Power of your Supermind: Vernon Howard

Online

You can email me anytime to discuss the Principles:
damiansmyth@btopenworld.com
My own company website can be found at: www.3ptraining.biz
or www.stressmanagementcoaching.co.uk

A superb resource for Principles training and movies can be found at:
www.threeprinciplesmovies.com

Further recommended online viewing:
www.inspiringcommunity.org/threeprinciples
www.three-principles.com
www.threeprinciplesresearch.com
www.threeprinciplesfoundation.org
www.3phd.net
www.sydneybanks.org
www.centerforsustainablechange.org
www.sccgov.org
www.3principlescoaches.com
www.starconsultancy.com
www.pranskyandassociates.com
www.insightprinciples.com
www.onethought.com
www.garretkramer.com
www.thethreeprinciples.blogspot.com
www.threeprinciplestraining.com
www.amichen.blogspot.com
www.healthrealize.com
www.threeprinciplesunlimited.com

Be connected
(or how to further your understanding of the Principles)

Listen (Syd Banks Audios)

All available from www.lonepinepublishing.com

Attitude! (CD–Audio);

Great Spirit, (CD–Audio);

Hawaii Lectures (CD–Audio);

In Quest of the Pearl (CD–Audio);

Long Beach Lectures (CD–Audio);

One Thought Away (CD–Audio);

Second Chance (CD–Audio);

Washington Lectures (CD–Audio);

What is Truth? (CD–Audio)

Watch (Syd Banks Videos)

All available from www.lonepinepublishing.com

The Hawaii Lectures (DVD);

#1 – Secret to the Mind,

#2 – Oneness of Life,

#3 – The Power of Thought,

#4 – Going Home

The Long Beach Lectures (DVD);

#1 – The Great Illusion,

#2 – Truth Lies Within,

#3 – The Experience,

#4 – Jumping the Boundaries of Time

The Experience (DVD)

Notes
(Just enough room for some insights!)

Printed in Great Britain
by Amazon